ONOMATOPEE 171

CO-MACHINES: MOBILE DISRUPTIVE ARCHITECTURE

ON/OFF
Dan Dorocic,
Kim Dovey
Nick Green
Mimi Zeiger
Fiona Shipwright
Michael Maginness
Alison Hugill
Diane Barbé
Samuel Días Carvalho
Benjamin Foerster-Baldenius
Ane Crisan
Halina Rachelson
Josh Plough
Melissa Jin
Ahmad S. Khouja
Kaegh
The Office of Urban Play
Tyler Stevermer
RealLabor
Marius Gantert
Office for Political Innovation
PINKCLOUD.DK
Philipp von Hase
Marcos L. Rosa

ConstructLab
SolidOperations
Íñigo Cornago &
Claudia Sánchez
Rachel Peachey & Paul Mosig
Precious Plastic
Guerilla Architects
Jason Vigneri-Beane
Karin Blomberg
Joel Kerner Tal Mor Sinay
Andrea Orving
Atelier Slant
Alex v. Lenthe
Takehito Etani
The Interactive Architecture Lab
Julia Klauer
Alex Bruce
Atilla Ali Tan
Leonard Daisuke Yui
Sahoko Yui
Niklas Fanelsa
place/making
Stefanie Rittler
Jan Bernstein
Carole Frances Lung

D1730912

ONO MATO PEE   ONF

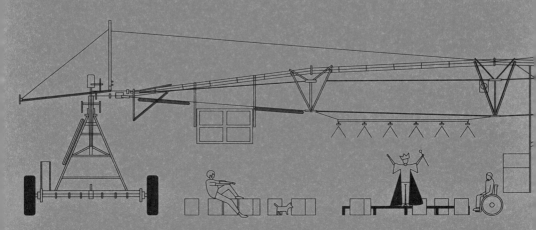

Stuck somewhere between an anthology and a catalogue this book relocates the definition of architecture and its role in contemporary cities. With their origins in ON/OFF's interdisciplinary design studio, the original Co-machines were an attempt to explain, codify and investigate the public spaces and streets of Berlin.

Now a global movement, this handbook collates, investigates and classifies the varied modes of practice that have developed around disruptive architecture. What's clear is that there is a group of designers and architects eschewing the more ossified elements of their practices in favour of nimble, critical and community lead interventions.

What this book demonstrates is that being stuck in-between something isn't a necessarily a bad place to be. The Co-machines bridge ideas and peoples. They show us that being "in-between" can be transformative. What does it mean when a group of designers or architects start illegally hustling beer on the streets (ON/OFF's Discospäti) or open a pizzeria in front of house to support the creative work happening in the back (Sugarhouse Studios by Assemble, which functioned through the summer of 2012); or making a mobile city kitchen (Íñigo Cornago & Claudia Sánchez p.124); opening a co-working design studio in a caravan trailer (Guerilla Architects p.126); creating Mechinvaders that provide infrastructure for protestors (Jason Vigneri-Beane, p.158) or occupying themselves with breeding chickens in shopping carts (Stefanie Rittler and Jan Bernstein, p.112)?

With reflections from a host of designers, writers, tinkerers and theorists the Co-machines demonstrate that the critical capacity of any creative project is best achieved through repeated making, deployment, reaction and re-deployment. In the form of Pamphlets these reflections explore subjects like surveillance, gentrification, and the legality of public interventions. They, like the machines themselves, don't provide easy answers. They contextualise them, acting as their replacement city streets as they've been removed from their natural habit and brought onto the pages of this book.

Now in its second edition, this publication and its authors have had a chance to look back on the past four years and grapple with the Co-machines and their close association with words like "maybe" and "potential. But it's mainly through use that these machines gain significance. So we urge you when reading this handbook to put it down, go outside, and build a Co-machine with a more curious mind.

CONTENT

WHAT IS A CO-MACHINE?

Dan Dorocic

9

We don't feel like we are represented in the city or that the city represents us, the inhabitants; and we don't want to work our way up the corporate ladder or work within the traditional system with its underlying structural problems; we don't agree with the stance of large corporations or private interests; we want to support the marginalised in our cities. We are pushed to act and to invent our own alternatives.

BERLIN AS A BREEDING GROUND

One aspect that has defined and moulded ON/OFF's work in the past years is the context of our local neighbourhoods in Berlin; especially the immigrant ones of Kreuzberg and Neukölln with their certain punk attitude and socialist politics. Living in these places and witnessing the city change over the years has defined the way we operate in it. For the entire time ON/OFF has functioned in Berlin it has been a city on the edge: the edge of becoming the lucrative German capital it was always meant to be.

The disappearance of the squats and the increasing rents, the opening of the fancy vegan restaurants on every corner and increased real estate speculation, when combined with the prevailing young, creative, anti-neoliberal attitude has made us dream about the possible alternatives of inhabiting our city, and not repeating the historic patterns of gentrification. Berlin's somewhat un-German character in the neighbourhoods of Kreuzberg and Neukölln has meant that its anti-establishment stance has rubbed off on our way of doing things. Berlin is itself a very disruptive city. Its complicated history of broken timelines has left scars and potential spots around the city for us to dream up these alternatives. But where we see change, developers see dollar signs.

So naturally we find ourselves in the age-old bind: to fight gentrification and top-down economic planning while simultaneously contributing to the gentrification by being artists that take over cheap workers' neighbourhoods. Our way of inhabiting these neighbourhoods is by adapting to the existing unregulated street culture you would see around Sonnenallee, and by promoting and bringing in new concepts of how to promote life on the streets that are anti-regulation. The physical Co-machines are just one of the more visible parts of this way of living and being. In the end, Co-machines are the outcome of many long conversations and invisible processes – some that challenged gentrification, some that fought for the rights of a community, and some for an alternative and sustainable existence.

Our often self-initiated mobile approach was for us the best way to interact with our adopted home city of Berlin. We got our inspiration not by designing homes, studios, and cafes for our creative friends, but by becoming active and responsive to predatory top-down city planning.

CO-MACHINES ARE BORN OUT OF NEED.

It's with access to resources, technology and time, that we've had the freedom to act in the city in the service of these alternatives. Is this the architecture of crisis? Is it a sustainable practice? The beginning of Co-machines started with such questions. They emerged from my own personal interests too, stemming from the beginning of my practice in architecture and with my practice within studio ON/OFF. Like many others before us, ON/OFF rejected what we saw as mainstream architecture practice to embrace our own design-build approach. Within this frame of practice we ran an open call under the name "Co-machines: Mobile Disruptive Architecture" in February 2016 to document the movement on a global scale. We wanted to take a break from the years of uninterrupted making, to take the time to reflect on the forces behind our process and to communicate and interrogate our actions as makers. This handbook is both the outcome of that desire and the response to the submission received from the open call.

The idea was to create a DIY guide, a legal rulebook and a how-to manual for inserting illegal or semi-legal micro-architectures in the city. But it quickly became clear that the complexities of each site and project meant that it would be very hard to transplant them, such is the nature of these local initiatives. Like exotic plants they can't simply be re-potted and expected to survive. Similarly, this kind of project doesn't perform well in a gallery or even in a book such as this one. They need to be experienced in their context, in motion, amidst their actions of disruption or subversion of public space. But the concepts they embody have a global tendency.

The open call wanted to "capture and explain how to make DIY, adhoc, hackable, movable, microtectures" for the future "Co-city". And the Co-machines do this, but they also represent the important notions of collaboration, commons and community. The community around each Co-machine provides the social agenda and urgency for its design. I have had numerous conversations with colleagues about the importance of these large-scale maps and the larger urban context around the point of attack of the Co-machine. We have to remember that the machines in this book are not stand-alone objects but the physical manifestation of 'projects', while many act as 'projectiles' to express a movement or thought. The original Co-machines book came out of a need to reflect on this specific "disruptive" DIY approach and to look wider to other cities and contexts for parallel practices. And as one question led to another, so this book is meant to lead to more.

The idea of taking to the streets with your soapbox and megaphone, to hustle for a buck, or to make a living by ad-hoc means are not new concepts, of course. Protestors, food-vendors, subsistence workers, street-performers, musicians, the traveling theatre, circuses, carpenters and others have been at it for millennia. What's interesting here is that many creative workers, especially in Berlin, are choosing this as a preferable way of working. The flipside to this is that the movement is also becoming rapidly normalised and used by the state. Since the financial crisis of 2008, governments and developers have become accustomed to relying on artists and designers to take on social, cultural and educational work that would otherwise be assumed by the welfare state. Many of these kinds of projects are presented as social work done voluntarily by a creative, underfunded group.

A reference for this book is the work of the numerous design collectives we collaborate with, have worked with or looked to for inspiration over the past decades; such as raumlaborberlin, exyst, Todo por la Praxis (TXP), Studio Weave, Baupiloten, and older collectives like Haus-Rucker-Co, Ant farm, Rural studio, Archigram and Super-studio, just to name a few. Another credit for this book is Atelier Bow Wow's Pet Architecture Guide Book project, which embraces the complexity of Tokyo's changing cityscape and interstitial spaces. It documents the buildings that have squeezed themselves into left-over spaces while also creating a guide to show the small, "cute" pet-architectures that can be found all around Tokyo. Similarly, the Co-machines are animals as architecture that run through our city streets. It's precisely because they move and hide that they're not easy to map.

So what are Co-machines? Are they public art? What makes them architecture? Is it the mobility that defines them? Is it their illegality? Is it the fact that they're part of a larger political movement? I cannot give you those answers, simply. The Co-machines project has become a research project cataloguing specific interventions around the world, to show that the local does have a connection to the global. It paints a movement that is still in its infancy. Co-machines are low-budget, often analogue, cheaply built, re-appropriating ready-mades such as shopping carts, bikes, and even irrigation systems, or incorporating very low-tech solutions. Yet they have to be clever in their design, sturdy, and easy to use and understand. They are in many ways the antithesis to the surveillance state, to the post-modern parametric surfaces and façades utilised by contemporary architects. Who knows how these analogue machines will adapt to future technology? Will they express in public space what

12 the virtual world is building? How will public space usage and commoning practices continue? How will Co-machines evolve? What we need to do is create better urban planning regulations and organise our cities to promote thriving & healthy public spaces for self-initiated projects, a (sub)culture of use and a political public life which the interventions in this book embody.

PS.:
At the time of writing this, the issue of Co-machines has even more of an urgency for us. We are not only marginalised and polarised by algorithms on social networks, coerced to only interact with like-minded people. But we are now in the middle of the COVID-19 pandemic, which is physically separating us into our own individual spaces. And even when we get the chance to inhabit public space we have stay in our physically policed invisible 2-3m bubbles. The 'Co-' in Co-machines stands for close social interaction, collaboration and action in public space. Sometimes we are labelled as practicing Social Architecture but we have argued that we practice the Architecture of Socialising, this means rubbing shoulders and encountering some social and political friction, which is now even more difficult. Being in the midst, and aftermath, of the 'quarantine' or 'shelter-in-place' we can look at this book and reflect on the struggles behind each Co-machine: Whose movement in public space is restricted, who inhabits the city now, what sorts of controls and regulations are being put into place to stop and make public action more illegal, and who would this serve? The Co-machines are machines of crisis, and a means of responding to regulation policing public space. So I for one predict, on the other side of this mess, that there will be a bloom of Co-machines inhabiting our cities.

Real existing communities develop shared priorities
and shared skills as well as, of course, conflicting approaches
to the uses of urban space.
- The City as Commons, Stavros Stavrides

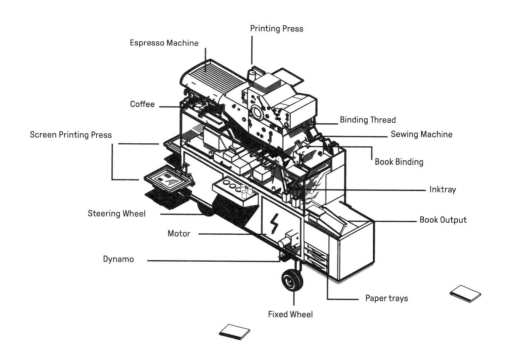

Printing Press
Espresso Machine
Coffee
Binding Thread
Screen Printing Press
Sewing Machine
Book Binding
Inktray
Steering Wheel
Book Output
Motor
Dynamo
Paper trays
Fixed Wheel

**GUERRILLA PRINTING PRESS
CO-MACHINE
No. 899,050,016**

The mobile Guerrilla Printing Press as imagined
as part of the International Co-machines Open Call

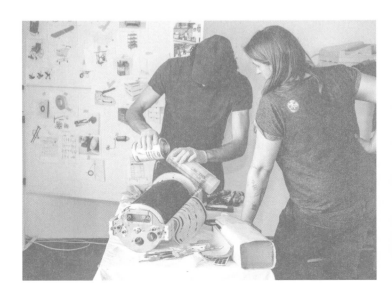

The mobile Guerrilla Printing Press as actually executed
at the Bauhaus Summer School in 2016 in Dessau.

WHEELS WERE THE ANSWER, BUT WHAT WAS THE QUESTION?

Samuel Días Carvalho

There are two important factors at play here. One is that ON/OFF was founded in early 2012, four years into the 2008 financial crisis. So we were starting our trajectories in a economic environment where there was not a lot of building going on. The other factor is Berlin, where it was cheap to live, giving us the freedom to self-initiate projects and experiment in public space. It's important to state too, that we all had a background and strong interest in art and "action", and the city certainly amplified this.

Our first project was the Kopf Kino. It was our collective's birth and the Istanbul Design Biennale was our baptism of fire. The idea of the Kopf Kino was to build a tool or machine that moved around our neighbourhood, captured people on camera and projected them onto these large blank facades that are prominent in Berlin. An amplifier that would allow people to perform in their city. We built it using a stolen shopping cart, borrowed car batteries and a projector and took to the streets. We applied to the Istanbul Design Biennale and got selected to show the project there.

Not comfortable with the idea of just exhibiting a film or the object we convinced the curators to allow us to travel to Istanbul and run some actions there. This was a very important moment for us as a group, to experience Istanbul together; building a new Kopf Kino with the local craftsmen of Kadiköy and running the action in the streets of Istanbul while filming the process to exhibit at the Biennale.

After that experience we started developing other projects that moved in the city and interacted with the public. At the time, due to austerity and the lack of work, there were many design collectives popping up throughout Europe (I limit myself to Europe as it's the space we worked and know best) working in public space and with participation, which was a very interesting wave to witness. Of course there were some pioneers and early constellations in the late 90's like exzyt and raumlabor (who it should be noted, many of us worked for). But after 2008 one had the impression that this movement had grown significantly. Although, I think we were slightly different to the majority of these groups—which might explain our lack of visibility—as most of them worked with participation and co-building, whilst we were more interested in designed objects, mobility and "performance".

When we deployed our objects audience "disruption" was the goal. So for us it has always been about shifting the roles of the audience, performer, consumer etc. What we were interested in was to temporarily suspend reality and test set roles through playful objects and typologies. But the playfulness had a political significance to it and that's when we started introducing the word "disruptive". Due to the normative nature of public space, we were always breaking some certain law, protocol or convention, which usually involved some exchange with power structures and the subsequent negotiations.

So these projects and objects, (and this circles back to the beginning when describing Kopf Kino as a tool), were always built to test and measure the temperature of shared space; a barometer of how people act in public space with its limitations and potentials. There was no object being collectively built, we had already previously done that. It was the experience of the object that mattered and what that told us about a space.

A mobile Fireplace in the Ermine Estate, Lincoln, UK (2020)
photo credit: Fergus Carmichael and Mansions of the Future

The Music-playing PINGBall in Vejle 2019

The Music-playing PINGBall in Vejle 2019

Inflatable City Hall 'Great Escape' Denmark 2016

ON/OFF'S START: THE KOPFKINO

Since 2012 along with more regular architectural practice, ON/OFF have been developing the idea of self-initiated or bottom-up interventions to develop new uses and ways to interact and play in city streets and parks. It all started with the Kopfkino which is a mobile monolithic urban life amplifier.

The KopfKino idea was to activate the potentials of our urban setting; the blank facades, the busy streets, the characters that comprise what we understand as our community and our city.

The Kopf Kino has been exhibited during the 2012 Design Biennal in Istanbul, Art Spin Berlin, the 2016 Venice Design Biennale, Wired Festival in Milano and has furthermore rolled through the cities of Sarajevo, Birmingham, Berlin, Frankfurt and Mannheim, Helsinki, Gothenburg, Kolding and Bergen.

The original KopfKino was designed in 2012 by Berk Asal, Sam Carvalho & Nicholas Green and has been adapted by other members of ON/OFF many times.

The Original 2012 Kopfkino taking Public Transport in Berlin

A 2019 Version of Kopfkino developed
in Gothenburg, Sweden

A version of the Kopfkino clad in Venetian Advertising
Posters built and deployed for the Venice Architecture
Biennale in 2016

A reflective Koprkino developed and built in Denmark in 2017

A later curved aluminum version of the Kopfkino specifically developed for the city of Bergen, Norway in 2020

PAMPHLETS

INTRODUCTION: MURMURS

Mimi Zeiger

> My dream is a movement with such deep trust that we move
> as a murmuration, the way groups of starlings billow, dive, spin,
> dance collectively through the air.
> —adrienne marie brown[1]

A little more than a decade ago, I first began tracking an expanded field of projects and practices of the kind explored in *Co-Machines*. It was during some of the darker days of the global recession previous to our own, when many young designers, unemployed due to rapidly downsizing firms, had a lot of time on their hands.

One Saturday afternoon, I stood in a vacant lot in Brooklyn, surrounded by a mini-golf course, each hole by a different local designer, each design in need of work. An urbanism culled from precarious conditions, this grassroots effort suggested that play, not problem-solving, was at the heart of the movement. Later, I would come to recognise the import of the "tactics", via Michel de Certeau, embodied in this work—a politic that could dive and spin to react to the moment, and yet might also scatter or dissipate under neoliberal pressures.

Unable to find a single term to categorise this trend of small-scale and self-commissioned projects, I used many, subtitling a 2011 piece written for Places Journal: *Provisional, Opportunistic, Ubiquitous, and Odd Tactics in Guerilla and DIY Practice and Urbanism*. "With this verbaciousness, I hope to capture the tactical multiplicity and inventive thinking that have cropped up in the vacuum of more conventional commissions."[2], I wrote at the time.

Dumpster pools, pop-up parks made from shipping pallets, and scrappy mini-golf courses offered a glimmer of hope to a profession that seemed to be imploding. The rapid-fire, on-the-street character of these projects held an immediacy and accessibility different from the paper architecture that had defined earlier recessions. Paired with a second trend, the mid-2000s rise of pro-bono architecture and design in service of communities in need, often overseas, there seemed to be an overall sea change within the field.

Over the years, I've watched the fields of art and design take a more generous position, with the expanding acceptance of social practice and social-impact design. In 2013, the *New York Times* noted the trend, writing:

35

Known primarily as social practice, its practitioners freely blur the lines among object making, performance, political activism, community organizing, environmentalism and investigative journalism, creating a deeply participatory art that often flourishes outside the gallery and museum system. And in so doing, they push an old question — "Why is it art?" — as close to the breaking point as contemporary art ever has.[3]

Seven years later, that old question is moot. Galleries, museums, art fairs, and biennials have largely integrated these projects into their public programming and funding structures. But the topic of "social" practices within architecture and design rather than "social practice" in fine art is sprawling, with patchy criteria for inclusion. How to define such a category, especially over time? Isn't all architecture at one point or another social? To define an architect's mindfulness to communities, political affiliations, fights for justice, or hopes for equity, almost always intimates a social-versus-formal binary trap and risks positioning a practice along a spectrum that runs from a-formal to anti-disciplinary.

So, while for some practitioners, the critical rejection of form and discipline is necessary as a clear oppositional break. For others, what seems like a deliberate turn is more of an organic shift towards the edge and beyond compelled by economics, personal values and interests, and opportunity. And both represent a larger turn within architecture—a growing murmur that, while not new, embodies certain dissatisfactions with the discipline's internalised mores. Something made critically clear by the pandemic and Black Lives Matters.

Co-Machines, as laid forth by Dan Dorocic in this volume and especially with an emphasis on mobility and disruption, occupy a category both overlapping and in-between the pop-up and the pro-bono. The connective tissue draws on sociability, social-agency, and social-mindedness. These are works and ideas that bring people together, offer subjectivity for designer and audience alike, and operate in service of a larger common good.

These two threads of practice share interest in serving a wider set of clients and transdisciplinary imaginaries. And both have weathered criticism as to efficacy and methodology: Who are these projects serving? Should designers heroically "parachute in" to arenas that would be better served by grassroots organising, policy changes, or humanitarian outreach? And, of course, Where's the form? These questions, which, despite a more mainstream embrace, continue to keep more social practices at the disciplinary fringe.

36 But perhaps such critiques are out of date. The aesthetic language of Co-machine interventions coalesces around DIY technique and materials, which is also itself an ethos, as well as a delight. Projects address the complexity of the city vis-à-vis the human subject. Architecture and the body are aligned agents.

Today, these designs and practices resonate with the need to redefine civic space in light of COVID-19 and the global recognition of systemic racism. Indeed, within the small-scale efforts to introduce everyday architectures into the city, there are retrospective echoes of discourses around care and mutual aid. How might a Co-machine architecture, not at-risk laborers, Amazon drones, or fleets of autonomous robots, navigate the space of the social—that territory between the self and the boundaries of the state or private development?

As I look out to the near and distance future, from the uncertainties of our contemporary, a present that mirrors uncertainties of a decade ago, I find solace in how here in my hometown of Los Angeles, as well as places across the globe, front yard art exhibitions and parking lot drive-in performances, for example, have cropped up like mushrooms after a storm. Dynamic inventions with porous points of entry for broad audiences. This is a nascent set of *Co-Machines* full of potential to reflect upon a decade from now. I imagine these empathetic designs moving through the city with the fleetness of starlings to replace the monument and the master plan.

1   Adrienne Maree Brown, *Emergent Strategy: Shaping Change, Changing Worlds*. Chico, CA: AK Press, 2017. P.71.
2   Mimi Zeiger, "The Interventionist's Toolkit: 1," *Places Journal*, January 2011. Website accessed October 24, 2019. https://doi.org/10.22269/110131
3   Randy Kennedy, "Outside the Citadel, Social Practice Art Is Intended to Nurture", The New York Times, March 20, 2013. Website accessed, August 16, 2020. https://www.nytimes.com/2013/03/24/arts/design/outside-the-citadel-social-practice-art-is-intended-to-nurture.html

TEMPORARY AND TACTICAL

Kim Dovey

Temporary and tactical interventions in public space have become a key urban design trend of the 21st century. Such projects range from guerrilla gardens, crosswalks, parklets and bike lanes through to more formalised temporary beaches and swimming pools, instant plazas, pop-up buildings, food trucks, mobile architectures, outdoor theatres, and container towns. This emerging field of practices is difficult to define but can be described as an intersection of the interim and the interstitial. It is variously termed 'temporary urbanism', 'insurgent urbanism', 'urban catalyst', 'tactical urbanism', 'austerity urbanism', 'DIY urban design', 'pop up urbanism' and 'guerrilla urbanism'. This is a broad field of incremental urban transformations that fill interim periods of time and underutilised spaces: the vacuums and terrains both vague and smooth. They are often cyclic, taking advantage of the daily, weekly and seasonal rhythms that produce times of underuse and the economic downturns that yield cheap or vacant space.

The idea of tactical urbanism links to the theories of Certeau and Deleuze, in which a tactic is an action that takes place within a context that may be antithetical; a rhizomic movement within a tree-like strategy. Tactical urbanism is a poaching operation, a form of encroachment. But tactics are also productive in that they seek to discover and create potentials and possibilities out of latent capacities. The temporary and tactical involves a creative engagement with the capacities and possibilities of the everyday city, a refusal to accept the seeming permanence of the existing structures. While temporary transformations terminate by definition, they may also morph into something new. In many cases, a temporary transformation becomes permanent over time. Temporary/tactical urbanism works within the existing urban infrastructure, adapting and transforming existing types such as car parks, containers, vehicles, and trees. It works within, around, and against existing practices and regulations. There is much to admire in many of these temporary projects: pioneering enterprise, social commitment, a spirit of adaptation, exploitation of new materials and technologies, and urban greening strategies. This is a call to understand the city as a place under constant revision with room to move and space for

39 the unexpected; where temporary opportunities are taken with high levels of creative community engagement and design collaboration. While these dynamic new forms of urban design are worth celebrating, they also raise important questions about power, agency, and public interests. Tactics for temporarily filling urban voids can be seen as well-adapted to the cycles of creative destruction that characterise neoliberal urban development. Is this just cheap urban design for periods of austerity, where artists and activists collaborate with out-of-work architects and urbanists to fill the gaps created by capitalist markets as an interim between permanent projects? What happens to design quality when we think a project is temporary, only for it to become permanent? Temporary/tactical urbanism is clearly geared to the failures of market capitalism, particularly high rates of vacancy and dereliction. There is also the sense in which the temporary and tactical is an integral part of advanced capitalism, creating a word-of-mouth 'buzz' and heightened demand. To what degree can temporary projects facilitate the privatisation of public space through advertising and commerce? Urban events are increasingly used to generate brand identity for both places and products; it can become difficult to distinguish creative temporary urbanism from a camouflaged marketing campaign. The temporary activation of public space can also be a 'band-aid' solution deployed to produce political capital and obscure the larger failures of urban planning. These new forms of agile, innovative, and self-organised urban design can be used to legitimatise the state's withdrawal from urban planning and investment. The movement towards this type of urbanism can be construed as an informalisation of the overdetermined cities of the global north. In this regard it is a counterpoint to the informal cities of the global south where the temporary and tactical has been a primary mode of urbanisation for over fifty years. This is apparent in the informal settlements that fill the interstices and margins of the formal city, and in the informal trading that encroaches onto public space. As divisions between the global north and south dissolve, these relations between formal and informal urbanisms become more complex. The temporary and tactical are often in tension with the permanent and strategic, yet they are also in a process of becoming what they challenge.

CO-MACHINES: ARCHITECTURE AND IMMEDIACY

Nick Green

When we talk about cities we are describing something incredibly complex, something multi-scalar, the sum of multiple layers of economies, built fabrics, communities, in many cases vast histories, as well as everyday moments; life being played out. It isn't so surprising, then, that there are a number of paradoxes inherent in the idea of the 'city'. For example, it is at once true to say that cities are vehicles of the powerful, shaped by the dominant interests of a period, as well as to assert that they are fundamentally collective creations, an ensemble of lived experiences. Understanding the city as such helps us to describe Co-machines; interventions not solely born out of resistance, but also the result of curiosity and the pursuit of desire. Their importance is maintained regardless of their genesis because, in every case, Co-machines seek to provide their creators with a tool to explore and engage with the city. Perhaps it is useful to consider the antithesis to the Co-machine—the Me-machine?— and to expand further on what is meant by the word. I would suggest that the archetypal Me-machine, particularly in relation to cities, is the car. Cars are, of course, highly specialised machines, designed to enable journeys between destinations without compromise. They are inward-looking, shielding their passengers within and presenting their curvaceous and unassuming metallic skin to the street. The car is a tool of self-interest and its supporting infrastructure—the roads, junctions, freeways, and by-passes— have taken precedence over the pedestrian, human-scale spaces of our cities. Co-machines whether ad-hoc or carefully planned— are low-tech, constructed by those hoping to utilise them. They are built specifically to engage with their context, to amplify and distort the relationship between their users and the city. Co-machines want to be seen and want to say something, and whether dialogues are fleetingly or are more sustained, their function is to catalyse something collective at street-level.

41	The car springs to mind as an opposite of the Co-machine partly because its relationship with the city is based predominantly on movement. Whether on wheels, tracks, floating or dragged by sheer force, Co-machines are also mobile interventions. They have a trajectory through the city, which in itself is propositional. Deciding upon an alternative route of action through urban space—for example, traversing a street, path, a shopping centre and into the communal garden of a housing estate— can create momentary relationships between territories often separated. The public has a right to access the benefits of the city, but understanding what that might entail is an issue rarely explored. Co-machines and the associated actions of deploying them in the city bring into sharp focus some of these latent potentials; spontaneity and surprise, a conflict or a connection. As these objects make their way between neighbourhoods, the space of the city is tested, an alternative use can render visible actors so far unappreciated or unnoticed.

It is interesting to ask whether Co-machines could be called architecture. Returning to the idea of power shaping the city, architecture is among the principal means of achieving this. While architecture can be civic and it can embody publicness or express a generosity to the street, it is principally procured and controlled by those with the most power. Does the ephemeral nature of Co-machines allow them to become a direct architecture, built and utilised by amateur-experts to test and play with the space of their city? I would suggest yes. They are experiments and excursions into the complex layers of the urban experience and while they are perhaps short-lived, they assert architecture in a different role, that of challenging the dominant power. For those who believe we all have a right to the city, we must consider what the responsibility of architecture is in enabling that right. Rather than thinking of architecture simply as a backdrop to everyday life or the structure inhabited by it, why not a direct-architecture that does not suggest, or hint at, communality, but which is enacted and utilised to generate something collective.

42 HOPE IN THE ERROR

Fiona Shipwright

There is a Heiner Müller quote that I find myself returning to again and again: "Die einzige Hoffnung sind die Fehler, die Zufälle - das, was nicht funktioniert. Wenn diese technologischen Systeme funktionierten, sind wir verloren."[1] ["...the only hope is in error because when all the technological systems work - we are lost."] This moment of error—whether represented through the cease of functioning or the interruption of a function—or, put more simply, the glitch, is something I have thought about a lot in relation to the ever-pervasive discourse of the "smart city". In this explicit co-joining of technology with architecture, I find myself fascinated by the notion of the "architectural glitch"; namely just what the term might refer to and the possibilities afforded by such a space.

Perhaps space is a misnomer: it seems more fitting to speak of "gaps". Given all this, as I reflect on the collection of Co-machines— "dreammachines from the future"—and the technology and strategies they give life to, the word machine should perhaps give cause for concern. Maybe it's worth taking pause and considering the difference between a machine, and the frame through which we tend to look at and define the discourse of the smart city and the notion of hacking that accompanies it. Assemble member Giles Smith—prior to the Turner Prize-winning activities of the collective—who in their practice seek to "address the typical disconnection between the public and the process by which places are made", wrote an MA dissertation on glitch architecture, in which he observes that:

> "Contemporary Architecture exists symbiotically with the digital. The narrative of the architect's relationship with technology has collided with the character of the architect in the form of the computer: a tool that has achieved the most radical revolution of the architect's own working processes since the invention of perspective. This conflict with the thinking-machine is the source of much contemporary anxiety in an architect's practice, and yet also much possibility."[2]

43 Within that, I think, lies the true concern for the Co-machine: it doesn't pertain to a fear of the error of the Co-machine; rather, it comes down to the danger of the machine that works too well. Nowadays, the machine regarded as functioning "best" is that which you are unaware of, that which you cannot see. Taken to its furthest extreme, it is even that which you cannot discern as being something distinct from the context within which it operates. Operating at the vastest of scales, the prerequisite of the "smart city" is to hide everything that makes an entire city run so "smartly", to place behind the bonnet and render less visible the mechanisms of its machinery. In this respect, the smart approach at this scale mirrors that of the consumer tech world, where the machine is also required to become discrete and unseen, to "just work". Here, one is constantly encouraged to eschew troublesome questions about just how it might work. It's interesting to note, too, that the product interfaces of consumer techland often borrow the language of architecture in order to make sense of the ephemeral and abstract concepts upon which they are built or conceived to further propagate. We navigate between "windows", we spend time in online "spaces" (once more commonly referred to as chat "rooms"), we protect things behind fire "walls", and programmers work with technical "architectures" to enable the smart city. It does not, however, follow that we should borrow the sensibilities of the digital when it comes to city making. Despite the best attempts of various marketing strategies to convince otherwise, you can't actually download the city of the future. Hacking the city doesn't mean so much either when such attempts are limited to endeavours meticulously tracked in isolation on individual handsets. Having it all down in digital form does not, in fact, negate the need to actually get onto the street. In order to address and take on the environmental, economic, and social issues that this volume highlights, Co-machines need to be in some sense visible. But how to do so in a world where the sought after ideal is one seamlessly-integrated-coherent-system? Easy: try working not as well. As Adam Greenfield has noted in his critique of the smart city: "The smartest cities rely on citizen cunning and unglamorous technology." Speaking of sites such as Occupy Sandy distribution centres as well as Madrid's el Campo de Cebada, he also notes that:

> "...the sustaining interactivity was for the most part founded on the use of mature technologies, long de-glamorised and long settled into what the technology-consulting practice Gartner refers to as the 'trough of disillusionment'."[3]

44 That de-glamourising process is changing too. After all, Swiss architecture practice Gramazio Kohler have been using drones to build walls for several years now. Those same drones will shortly begin delivering Amazon packages. Those same drones are being unwrapped on Christmas day. Those same drones are being used to take your wedding photos. And those same drones are policing the streets of France and China. A lot of people now already have their very own "machine", but there's not much "co" about it. The technology we inherit, that has been stripped of its glamour, is increasingly advanced but is also increasingly individualistic. A stand-alone bit of kit only connected in the sense that it's plugged in to the corporate networks of the smart city. For this reason, now is the time to establish and make explicit the practice of the Co-machine, not the individual machine.

Let the Co-machines be on the ground, working in and making visible those gaps left by error. Such interventions work best when they stay within the eyeline of those they intend to serve or help: people. We must prioritise the human view without being taken in other directions, out of sight. Be that way up high above (the drone-eye view), or far below (hidden underneath the bonnet of the smart city), or into the ether (the ephemeral land of the app). The term machine in its commonest form refers to an "apparatus", one that employs mechanical power and several parts that function together to perform a particular task. It's also worth remembering that the term also has meaning within a political context: the notion of the "machine" as "an efficient and well-organized group of powerful people". Considering this in partnership with Müller's celebration of and hope for error, does this represent some kind of de Certeau-esque upgrade of Luddite philosophy? Not quite. It's not about breaking the machines themselves, it's about harnessing their capacity to act as collision machines, as contamination machines, as complex machines. In short, as machines capable of breaking something else. And so, all hail the new Geniale Dilettanten (the ingenious amateurs) of the digital age: the Co-machines.

1   Heiner Müller, "Warum zünden Sie keine Kaufhäuser an?", in *Gesammelte Irrtümer 2* (Frankfurt/Main: Verlag der Autoren) 1990, p.158.

2   Giles Smith, "A Glitch Architecture Possibilities Primer", MA dissertation thesis submitted in fulfilment of the MA Architecture course at the Royal College of Art, 2012, p.32.

3   Adam Greenfield, "The smartest cities rely on citizen cunning and unglamorous technology", in *The Guardian*, December 22, 2014: https://www.theguardian.com/cities/2014/dec/22/the-smartest-cities-rely-on-citizen-cunning-and-unglamorous-technology

ON/OFF mobile tensegrity playground project BOULEvard
in use in Brussels photo courtesy Tim Van de Velde

THE SPACE FOR COMMUNITY

Alison Hugill

According to urban sociologist Talja Blokland in her book *Community as Urban Practice*, the term community is widely used in this field because it has the convenience of being imprecise: "loaded with positive connotations" it describes a social body that few people would argue against. This imprecision gives the word a political currency, often halting further inquiry into the layers of structural difference and marginalisation at work in each community or locality. The term has also been used to bolster moral pleas for participation and social engagement spearheaded by governments and real estate developers hoping to normalise subsequent unilateral actions. For example, many interim-use architecture projects hope to bridge the gap between communities and corporations experiencing local back-lash for building plans, via a kind of architecture-as-social-work that paves the way for further exploitation. This is one possible fate of temporary, nomadic, and DIY design projects that remain at the level of fetishisation, rather than going deeper into the role that structural inequalities play in our everyday experience of the city.

In a recent ON/OFF project, commissioned by Mansions of the Future in Lincoln, UK under the programme heading "Urban Form: Social Architecture and the Commons," we were invited to think about the legacy of social housing developments defined by social democratic ideals, especially those in the local built environment. In response to this, we were pushed to consider how this practice of mobile, disruptive architecture figures into a history of social archi-tecture more broadly. The conclusion: Co-machines do not aim to find blanket solutions for social problems, in the vein of earlier tradi-tions of social housing or newer neoliberal models. Rather, the Co-machines represent an "architecture of socialising." By this, we mean that the objects and encounters initiated by these projects aim to disrupt or distort the usual flow of our urban lives by creating new kinds of social engagements and arrangements. They motivate people to critically reconsider the spaces and frameworks that they occupy and act within.

47 The resulting project—a Co-machine called 'Public House'—engaged with the history of the pub in the UK and its important role as a meeting place (originally in domestic spaces, inviting political discussion, mutual aid and organisation) as well as its role in contemporary society. Inverting the historical role of the Public House as a domestic space that invited the community in, we created a mobile, warm, home-like hearth that could be brought outside and through the streets. Pushing the mobile chimenea through the Ermine Estate on a cold February afternoon, we stopped at different sites along the way to talk about the changing landscape of the neighbourhood, what community spaces had been defunded or closed altogether, why that was the case, and what was leftover.

This is one example of how Co-machines can function as interrogative tools in our understanding of community. Their playful exterior and performative deployment can and should act as a cover for launching deeper, political discussions about how communities function, or don't. In light of the current health pandemic, as well as the long-standing pandemic of structural racism and white supremacy worldwide, these kinds of informal projects and venues are gaining momentum. As justice systems and governments seem to be failing their citizens, many are turning to mutual aid and grassroots organising as long-term alternatives. But there is also a very real risk that informal, temporary, nomadic or DIY architectural strategies will be co-opted to further justify governments and institutions divesting from their responsibilities.

In a 2016 article reflecting on the 15th Venice Architecture Biennale, curated by Chilean architect Alejandro Aravena, I asked: "Are these kinds of collectivizing initiatives still radical, or merely evidence of localized individuals and groups picking up the social tab?" Problems seem to arise when artists and architects conflate the public (or community) with the political. Public space, socially-engaged or community-driven design projects are often considered political by nature. Yet few of them address the given terms by which they operate: what defines a community? Who is the public? By focusing efforts at a local level, socially-engaged art and architecture initiatives often fail to imagine how the urban politics they embody can address structural economic, social and political problems on a global scale. When systems like the welfare state fail, grassroots, autonomous self-organisation rises from the ashes. As these kinds of projects become more ubiquitous, they can risk normalising and fetishising a pervasive lack of governmental assistance. How do Co-machines figure into, on the one hand, a history of largely innocuous socially-engaged art practice and, on the other hand, a legacy of informal design within radical protest movements? Furthermore, what forms of grassroots knowledge are they indebted to?

48 The role of Co-machines is to address the broader public for which they are built, often by attending to more generalised, reproductive concerns, like gardening, food, social gathering, or childcare. In many instances, their address may have a disruptive quality, rather than one of cohesion. The name "Co-machine" is thus somewhat of a misnomer: their slowness and attention to interpersonal care is anything but machine-like, and their physical form opposes automation of the contemporary "smart city" variety. As mechanisms or tools for community use, they are thus malleable and open-ended: just about as open-ended as the notion of "community" itself. Their greatest gift lies, then, in their potential to interrogate their own terms, and to access and reckon with the structural differences (other possible co's: conflicts, contentions, collisions) that make up our otherwise amorphous understanding of community.

THE PRACTICE OF THE COMMONS

Michael Maginness

"Men have dreamed of liberating machines.
But there are no machines of freedom,
by definition." - Michel Foucault

The political experience of the 1960s and 1970s continues to exert a significant influence on socially- and politically-motivated practitioners of the built environment. In a manner similar to the diverse movements of the western left in the decades surrounding the tumult of 1968, the contemporary global left is engaged in a process of experimentation as it attempts to develop a new form of emancipatory politics to replace one that has grown obsolete. A situation recently described by Alain Badiou as a 'historical interval'. As part of this process of experimentation, the Co-machine is directly indebted to the politically motivated spatial practice that developed in the decades immediately preceding and following 1968. Its focus on a collective project of mobility, disruption, immediacy, and performance recalls an incredibly diverse range of references from the period; the psychogeography and dérives of the Situationists, the humour-based 'terrorism' of the Spaßguerillas, the spatial media practice of Ant Farm and the DIY attitude of the Whole Earth Catalogue, to name just a few.

For the contemporary left, the current 'historical interval' involves a process of coming to terms with historical failure and, in this regard, the legacy of the 1960s and 70s is often assessed in terms of defeat. However, it may be more instructive to adopt a genealogical approach that privileges an assessment of historical affect. For example, the Autonomia movement, which arose from the radical student and worker activism in Italy during the 1970s, can be considered a characteristic example of the political movements of this period, due to its iconoclastic creativity and violent break from the orthodox left. However, in their assessments of the lasting ideological effects of Autonomia, Paulo Virno and Sylvère Lotringer have convincingly argued that the demands of the movement merely consisted of an anticipation of the social conditions of late-capitalism and the rise of immaterial labour. The movement was not inherently subversive in itself and "confused non-socialist demands (refusal

51 of work, abolition of the state) with a proletarian revolution." Accordingly, "Autonomia was a defeated revolution, to which the post-Fordist paradigm was the answer." This assessment could be considered equally valid for many of the radical political movements making similar demands in the same era, from the Situationists to the student movements of West Germany and the United States.

The indirect realisation of the period's radical social demands culminated in the post-Fordist political economy, in which, according to Lotringer, "surplus value is no longer extracted from labour materialized in a product, it resides in the discrepancy between paid and unpaid work –the idle time of the mind that keeps enriching, unacknowledged, the fruits of immaterial labour." Surplus value is extracted from the surplus knowledge originating in the creativity, adaptability, and resilience of the ill-defined 'multitude' that has replaced the traditional working class, whether or not this knowledge is the direct result of paid labour: "The multitude is a force defined less by what it actually produces than by its virtuosity, its potential to produce and produce itself." This development reveals the potential political risk of deploying a Co-machine as a social end in itself, rather than as a tool in the realisation of a broader political strategy. There is a very real danger that a Co-machine can be inadvertently operationalised as a 'gentrification machine,' as the collaborative creativity and knowledge it embodies becomes commodified in the built environment. There is a tendency to think of gentrification in binary terms, as a kind of invasion of capital into the urban commons. In fact, gentrification often proceeds as the result of the recognition of the desirability of an effective and diverse urban commons. However, it is a recognition that exists in a political-economic reality in which this desirability can only be realised as exchange value. Areas of the city that exhibit the values associated with a strong sense of apparent urban authenticity—a heterotopic cultural diversity, an informal and active street life, a rich sense of community and belonging— increasingly have the capacity to produce a surplus value that can be extracted through property speculation on domestic and commercial spaces adjacent to successful public spaces. In this way, these urban areas exhibit something akin to the 'virtuosity' of unpaid and immaterial labour described by Virno and Lotringer.

While these urban qualities are integral to a liveable and equitable city, they are not inherently subversive in their own right. The concern of a socially-orientated spatial practice for the quality, authenticity, and universal accessibility of public space is compromised when divorced from the political-economic reality of the relationship between public space and private property. When deploying a Co-machine we must remember that neither the machine itself nor

52 the act of its deployment is necessarily subversive. There is no object, architecture, or thing that is inherently radical or emancipatory. "There are no machines of freedom," according to Foucault, "it can never be inherent in the structure of things to guarantee the exercise of freedom. The guarantee of freedom is freedom." However, architecture and spatial design can have a real political potential when their intentions "coincide with the real practice of people in the exercise of their freedom."

Berlin-Friedrichshain, July 2016

A RESPONSE FROM THE FUTURE, NOW:

Michael Maginness

With the previous essay, *The Practice of the Commons*, I sought to place the Co-machine within a historical lineage of emancipatory spatial politics. In doing so, I engaged in the risky business of historicising the present, by explaining the concept of the Co-machine as the product of a 'historical interval' characterised by a cultural and political experimentation that harnessed the uncertainty following the Global Financial Crisis. This attempt to write history as it unfolded might be excused with hindsight. ON/OFF's early Co-machines, and the previous essay, were produced within a zeitgeist awash with a kind of violent hopefulness. However, it feels as though there has been a recent and significant shift in mood. Experimentation, iconoclasm and creative improvisation have given way to doubt, exhaustion and desperation.

In this context, the essay's comparison between the post-GFC moment of hopeful experimentation with the political movements of the 1960s and early 70s seems especially poignant. Certainly it is too soon to speak of our recent 'historical interval' in terms of defeat, nonetheless, if in 2016 the Left was engaged in a "process of coming to terms with [the] historical failure" of the twentieth century, then perhaps now we can begin to assess our recent past using the approach that "privileges an assessment of historical affect." I was afraid that the 'virtuosity' of Co-machines, and the precarious labour of the creative class that produces them, could render them 'gentrification machines'. Four years later, it seems pertinent to assess whether this warning was justified and whether we heeded it while rolling our machines through the streets of Europe.

A spirited grassroots movement against displacement and the aggressive commodification of housing and public space has long existed in Berlin, but over the past half a decade it has entered the political mainstream. I hope that ON/OFF's Co-machines have contributed informally to this imperfect and disjointed process of urban politics in Berlin. Their contribution is primarily pedagogical (and perhaps sometimes paternalistic); demonstrating to urban inhabitants the power their everyday actions and social interactions have in shaping the reality of their public spaces. To that end, we have had the good fortune of collaborating with Quartiersmanagements and other grassroots neighbourhood and arts associations. However, even these organisations have been shown to have an ambivalent relationship with gentrification. I can't help but feel that our Co-machines - and their successes - have been tainted by the processes I described in my original essay.

The Co-machine has many origins, but Kopf Kino is a special project in its intellectual genesis for ON/OFF. In 2012 the social fallout from the previous year's explosive politics of public space were still fresh - Occupy Wall Street, the Arab Spring, the London Riots. The first Kopf Kino was hacked together in a Neukölln apartment in response to the latent performative potential of an empty façade, the type of which is distinctly characteristic of Berlin. The city's empty spaces, resulting from wartime destruction and a post-war recovery stunted by the city's physical division, have become renowned as incubators of the city's informal creative activity. But this urban typology is being steadily filled in, as a construction boom responds to soaring property prices and Berlin "becomes the lucrative German capital it was always meant to be". On one of the most (in)famous of these sites - the so called 'Cuvrybrache' - a 'start-up campus' is being constructed, which will house, among others, the German headquarters of the Dutch multinational food delivery service/gig-economy employer Lieferando. Meanwhile, residential rents in the Rixdorf neighbourhood of Neukölln, where the Kopf Kino was born, have almost doubled since it first rolled onto the streets.

Of all ON/OFF's Co-machines, Disco Späti exhibits a particular conceptual honesty. It developed organically and opportunistically in response to the partyfication of the traditionally chaotic May Day (International Worker's Day) celebrations in Berlin-Kreuzberg. But it also stems from a real and selfish need; to raise money for the renovation of an old motorcycle workshop into a studio space in the midst of soaring Berlin rents. The project's equivocal nature is therefore clear. Disco Späti is itself a creative self-survival mechanism against displacement and part of the desire to secure our own precarious place as artists in the city. It also mirrors the changing face of Berlin's May Day, as the holiday has become institutionalised by the city's left leaning coalition government through the MyFest street party and political demonstrations have become smaller. Street vendors have become a staple of the day and quickly attract the attention of the police, who no longer have to deal with as much political agitation as past years.

It appears that Co-machines did not become the gentrification machines of my nightmares, but neither did they come close to the lofty goal of "resisting the commodification of space ... by developing an alternative to the destructive logic of private property." Rather they exist as a kind of warning system or 'canary in the

56 coal mine.' In relation to gentrification, they continue to be victims, as well as perpetrators, trapped in a cyclical urban process that has been described by the urban theorist Kim Dovey as 'place suicide.'

Berlin-Neukölln, June 2020

LOVELY MACHINES ON ANTHROPOMORPHISM, CYBORGS AND SYSTEMS

Diane Barbé

I like to think
(it has to be!)
of a cybernetic ecology
where we are free of our labors
and joined back to nature,
returned to our mammal
brothers and sisters,
and all watched over
by machines of loving grace.
— Richard Brautigan

In 1967, Richard Brautigan published the poem *All Watched Over by Machines of Loving Grace*, which promoted the idea of a cybernetic ecological utopia, consisting of a fusion of computers and organisms living in perfect harmony and stability. The title poem, quoted above, envisions a world where cybernetics has advanced to a stage where it allows a *return* to the balance of nature, and an elimination of the need for human labour. This underscores the myth of nature as a state of equilibrium, which has been disrupted and needs to be returned to. The core idea of cybernetics is to propose a scientific reading of behaviours as predictable, regular, determinate, that is: a treatment of all things (including biology) as an interconnected *system.* On many different levels, thinking in terms of systems that influence each other, that depend on each other, and that *can be mapped*, has underscored every aspect of modern thinking, particularly our place as humans within an ecosystem. As the scientific analysis of bodies and environments –"such a bloodless word", writes Joy Williams in *Ill Nature*– becomes the most powerful language that describes and deconstructs us, I find it crucial to look into our peculiar relationship with machines, those pseudo-animate objects which can move but cannot truly think, neither natural nor completely alien. Instead of looking from the human perspective onto the object, instead of talking of *our machines*, why don't we focus on who we are *for them*? If I were a dishwasher, who would my humans be? If I were a truck, who would my drivers and passengers be?

Would they just be drivers who can use me, penetrate me, and direct me around?

We tend to think of machines as tools that, fundamentally, help us make sense of the chaos of time passing. We, as humans, assemble matter in ways that help mark, measure, count, move and transform matter around us, and from these new outputs we construct thoughts that have a trace. But matter, of course, is never truly inert: even rocks move, evolve, erode. So, plunged into the complexity of all the processes that co-exist incessantly, unable to grasp or remember it all, we seek to build instruments that can help us shift the time scale that we operate on. I speak here of those objects that surround us in everyday life, mass-produced "things" which, following an interaction, will perform another action whose mechanisms are not at that moment controlled by the human, but rather are programmed through some form of code (usually electronic chips). Because a logic is engraved in the chip, it becomes predictable: if a certain input occurs, a certain output or chain of outputs will ensue. Not much can deviate from the printed circuit. Press a button, and the engine starts. There is something incredibly reassuring about predictability, because it allows us to form habits. We get used to machines functioning the way we intend, and we get used to systems (no matter how inequitable) that will *probably* give the same results over, and over, and over again. It helps us feel like the world is logical, coherent, and safe.

But what about deficiencies and errors? What about those aspects of machines that make them playful and fun and interactive? Suzanne Ciani, an experimental musician who pioneered sound synthesis with the instrument builder Don Buchla, has long sensualised technology by bringing forth its lovability. In 1979, she designed the soundtrack of the Xenon pinball machine, using modified recordings of her voice as well as electronic sounds from the Buchla synthesiser. She wanted to "think of the pinball as actually playing a piece [of music]", she explained. Each event in the game has its sound, its commentary. On the playfield, colourful bumpers and poppers kick the little metal ball, grunting and gasping. It's like poking at the guts of a big, futuristic, living machine. An organism. One that can talk, that can get the player excited and seduced. On the board, the picture of Xenon looks like the face of a goddess –smooth blue skin, large yellow eyes, high cheekbones. She has teeth and lips, and her ears are more akin to that of a fish. This humanoid face, coupled with the bizarre organs of plastic and metal in her belly, builds up an ambiguous attraction to Xenon. What makes her truly "energising", as the 1980 advert proclaims, is her unique voice. "Welcome to Xenon", she says as you put a quarter in the coin slot. She sounds soft, slightly metallic, but alluring. During the game, she will give you advice, and if you lose, her voice changes, sounding more masculine, as she teases you: "Try Xenon again!"

It's a strange relationship that develops. Inside of the guts of Xenon, a small ball races around, and its trajectory is unpredictable. Even in this enclosed space, the possibilities are endless. This is what makes the game a game: something escapes our control, and we frantically punch the flippers to try to steer the situation, knowing that we might lose. Ciani created most of her music with Buchla synthesisers, modular systems that use various types of inputs – electrical pulses that define the duration, frequency and envelopes of sounds–producing complex, spatialised sound outputs. But even after forty years of playing the instrument, she explained in a RBMA master class in 2016, she still gets surprises. There is no illusion of complete control: the relationship between this machine and this human is one that gets woven and muddled, like trying to build a new language without translators. Taking the instrument apart and mapping the paths, pipes and networks that make up its core can help understand the grammar; but seeing the whole as a whole, interpreting the signs produced by the machine eventually requires us to admit that the machine also interprets the signs that *we* make. Both agents make mistakes. Perhaps it is this randomness that is fascinating for us: it is not about using a machine to make a sound or a book or a coffee, but rather a collaboration: a serendipitous act of co-creation that won't necessarily turn out the way we intended it to.

CO-MACHINES IN EINDHOVEN

In the autumn of 2019, ON/OFF and the creators of three Co-machines were gathered by Onomatopee to discuss their concepts, exchange ideas, realise and activate their designs on the streets of Eindhoven. Some built their ideas for the first time. The Workshop participants were Takehito Etani, Melissa Jin, Basses Stittgen, Donghwan Kam, Gianni Laneri Deforné, Michael Maginness, & Dan Dorocic. For the Talk program the additional participants were architects and curators Arie van Rangelrooy, Niels Groeneveld, Tim Prins and Theo Tegelaers. On the following pages is the documentation from that event. After the action, these Co-machines were also part of and exhibition during Dutch Design Week later that year.

"But I'm not so worried about the end result as long as we're doing and then seeing what happens. You can shoot the arrow but don't have control over where it's going to hit."

Takehito Etani

"On some of the other screens you show drawings which are the result of the process of communicating with Onomatopee while developing the project. You don't know the people through communication, you only know one aspect of one other. By displaying these drawings that process is made visible, something that is normally......"

Theo Tegelaers

".....behind closed doors. So before coming here all my experiences with ON/OFF and Onomatopee have been through my computer screen. I didn't really know these people at all, I was only communicating through email. Even when I was obtaining all the material I was on Amazon or secondhand.com, so the images there are an expression of how this machine came to be. It illustrates this process that's hidden away." Melissa Jin

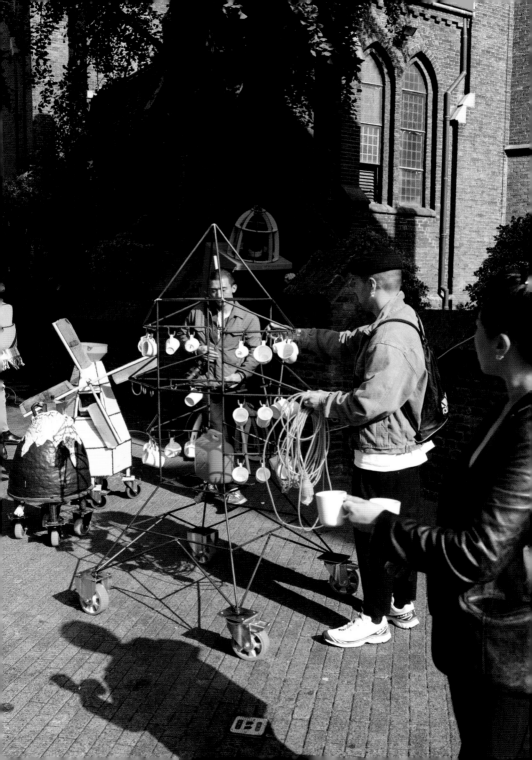

"We actually never described this project as a machine, but we were just contacted by Dan [Dorocic] and told that our project would be involved with Co-machines. Actually we still don't know if it's a machine or some playful object which has the ability to move around." Donghwan Kam

"I think playing is very important because when you're playing you're not really thinking so much about anything that's around you. You're just having fun and really having fun is what we try to do with this project. With the very simple action of grinding, we try to embody that in an object in a playful way. And through that get something out of it that is more than just using a coffee grinder." Basse Stittgen

"Of course we're all trying to get an underlying meaning, which we can do, but I hope tomorrow will be just fun." Donghwan Kam

"I think it's very important that as an individual you feel very comfortable in public and to also have a sense of ownership over space; in the sense that you have the freedom to do what you want to do."

Melissa Jin

"He's a sacred, gentle giant who connects heaven and earth. So this is the contraption that allows me to become the gentle giant, while also leaving footprints."

Takehito Etani

THE CO-MACHINES

Hortum Machina B

Mobile Re-Configurable Polyhedra

Transparent Footprints
of Invisible Giant Machines

Trolley Sound System

Mecha_A38
//Dark_Invader

Dance Vehicle 01

Precious Plastic

The Bicycle-Powered
Sewing Factory

Super Bob

Matroshka

The 100m Apparatus

Mobile Composter

Escaravox

Cocook Matadero

Exquisite Triciclo

Ch

The Garden
Goes Outside

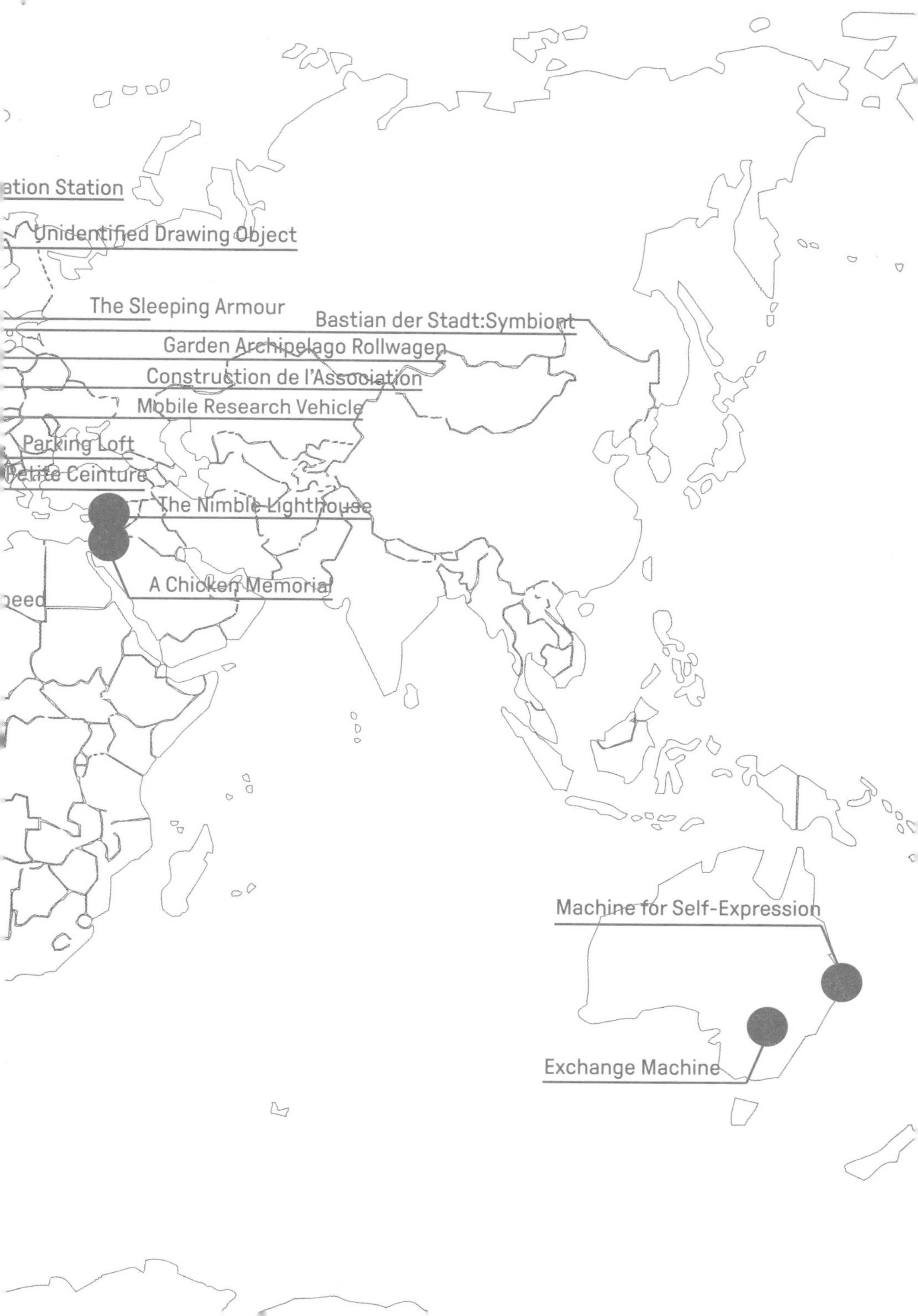

ation Station

Unidentified Drawing Object

The Sleeping Armour   Bastian der Stadt:Symbiont

Garden Archipelago Rollwagen

Construction de l'Association

Mobile Research Vehicle

Parking Loft

Petite Ceinture

The Nimble Lighthouse

A Chicken Memorial

eed

Machine for Self-Expression

Exchange Machine

THE LEGALITY QUESTION

Dan Dorocic

81 When you look at a Co-machine in the pages of this book, try to figure out why it looks the way it does. Is it an art project or a means of livelihood? Does it have an umbrella to shade from the sun, or to camouflage from the authorities? Does it mimic other street infrastructure, such as a garbage bin, or employ a street sign's aesthetics to remain undetected? Is it a manifesto in itself, a love letter, or is it an expression of interest? Does it amplify certain activities on city streets or does it try to prevent them? How does it evade being policed? Question the physical design outcomes to get at what is at stake in the thinking behind the decision- there is no such thing as a non-decision in design and 'lucky' accidents are very rare.

Co-machines react to their predominantly urban habitat. The modern city is planned in a grid in order to be easily secured and navigated. Traditional towns were planned along more organic roadways, with many nooks and hiding spots. These organic, traditional or "garden-plan" street logics made it easier to duck out of sight. Co-machines work to re-emphasise the city's voids, hiding in plain sight or at least operating in a way that static architecture simply can't. Throughout history, states have sought to control citizens through large urban planning actions under the guise of 'efficiency' and 'hygiene'. One such plan was spearheaded by Baron Haussmann, who proposed and succeeded in clearing large swaths of Paris to create large perpendicular boulevards that would cut through the existing organic streets. This modernist Haussmannian mania persisted through much of the 20th century, and acted to connect the larger city, but also took away the density and cohesion of localised communities. Another figure who wanted to implement this logic was Adolf Hitler's architect, Albert Speer. He wanted to demolish much of existing Berlin and in its place build a large boulevard and grand public buildings and nationalistic monuments to create the 'Welthauptstadt of Germania'. Luckily, this never came to be, although Soviets used similar tactics in East Berlin after WWII. At the end of the century, gaps and fields left behind from the removal of the Berlin Wall exposed ruined parts of the re-united city of Berlin. These became the environment for architectural and social experimentation.

The city of Berlin has had some success in using those gaps to its advantage to create great bottom-up community organised structures, common spaces rather than enclosures, where experimental and social experiments can proliferate. One example is Tempelhof Airport, built by the Nazis in WWII. Since its closure in 2008, the airfield has been used as a park, as a festival venue, a refugee center and for all sorts of artistic and design experiments. Co-machines are enacted or built by or with communities: they are the products of collaboration and co-ownership from different communities in the city and are, as such, usually deployed during protests, festivals or other such actions.

Generally speaking, however, contemporary cities and public spaces are not only designed and built to be hostile to loitering, but to homelessness, to animals, and skateboarders by having studs, spikes and cameras installed everywhere. They also have laws in place to prevent people from engaging with the city organically. When looking at the Co-machines in the pages of this book, we need to address their physical architecture and who they are for, which counter-intuitively includes mobility and urgency. As such, they are deployed with or without the minimal legal basis or regulatory backing. They generally need to break or bend rules in order to be able to operate in over-planned and over-policed public spaces. Many Co-machines are mobile exactly because of this, as they need to keep moving to evade official regulations.

Another big influence on Co-machines is their economic and environmental context. In contemporary consumer culture, the life-cycle of products and objects is short. They are discarded to landfills at alarming rates. However, in an economic, political, or health crisis, when it's more difficult for goods to cross borders, ingenuity kicks in and objects that are usually discarded are given a second life. One country that has been in a perpetual state of crisis since the late 1950s is Cuba. Its Co-machine inventions are a constant source of inspiration for the thinking behind this book. Leaking and rusted oil barrels are welded into a float or a barge; beaten-up cars and buses are brought back to life or converted into garden houses; a rotary telephone is engineered into an oscillating fan; a discarded fridge is repurposed into a mobile bar. Ready-made objects are not just thrown away, their embodied energy is repurposed to ingenious ends. Similarly, our Co-machines have their origins in crisis mentality, when artists and designers face an adverse economic reality and want to use their skills to self-initiate events and actions in public space. Is this type of ingenuity an inevitable effect of poverty or can it effectively be put into action to function in response to our low-energy, post-oil world?

The Co-machines also take cues from street vendors. And when one thinks of these, one can't ignore the fact that the urban architecture very much defines the structure of the Co-machine. For example, in Los Angeles - a city without pedestrians, the quintessential street vendor is a motorised vehicle, a Taco truck, that can take over a parking lot (the typical public space in a car-centered city) and can unfold plastic furniture on a street corner. For contrast in Bangkok, it is a wooden pushcart with a colourful umbrella that can navigate markets and busy pedestrian streets. In today's Berlin, a

European city in between these two, we feel like we have a choice to design.

A simple example comes from ON/OFF's work, the Discospäti. It's a mobile bar built from fridges we found discarded on the street that evades the law through its mobility and by sailing the grey waters of regulation. We have run this mobile bar in public spaces in Berlin for social events, May Day, carnival and fundraisers since 2014. In terms of legality, for the Discospäti we even took the extra step and tried to get a license, which doesn't exist. So we applied for the next best thing - a bike courier's licence at the Ordnungsamt (German regulatory office) and received a simple beverage vendor/delivery license that let us deliver refreshing drinks from a shop to a private residence/place. For operating as a vendor in public space, in Berlin and elsewhere, one must have a permanent "stand" or ownership of a private plot or space from which to sell goods. As such, no existing permit for a mobile vendor exists. During operations with the Discospäti when stopped by police, our delivery license was shown to confuse the authorities. In the worst case the operator received a warning, but the confusion let it escape to another street corner or its hiding spot. Artists and designers didn't invent this behaviour, this kind of tactical urbanism is widely used by street merchants, and is rejected by top-down regulating bodies in cities trying to control public space. You need to act in your city in order to save it from developers. You need to act in your city to stop it from becoming a generic shopping mall. You need to act in your city to prevent rising rents kicking people out of their homes. Get out there and take things into your own hands!

The Garden Goes
Outside

Exquisite Triciclo

Garden Archipelago
Rollwagen

Trolley Sound System

Frau Fiber and the Bicycle-
Powered Sewing Factory

Chicks On Speed

Mobile Research Vehicle

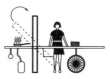

Cocook Matadero

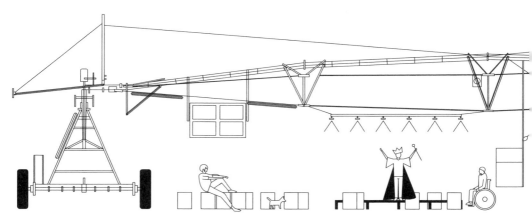

Bikecropolis
p. 100

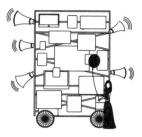

Machine for Self-Expression
p. 104

Unidentified
Drawing Object
p. 114

Exchange Machine
p. 118

Bastian der Stadt: Symbiont
p. 126

Creation Station
p. 128

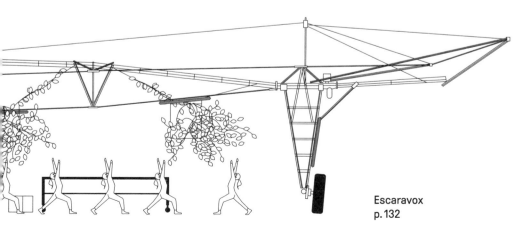

Escaravox
p. 132

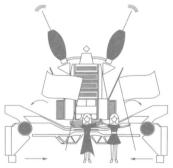

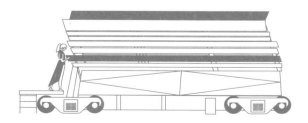

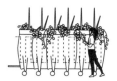

Mobile Composter
p. 140

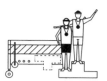

The 100m Apparatus
p. 142

Transparent Footprints of
Invisible Giants Machines
p. 150

Dance Vehicle 01
p. 152

A Chicken Memorial
p. 160

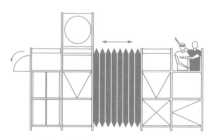

Parking Loft
p. 162

Hortum machina B
p. 168

Construction de
l'Association
p. 170

THE GARDEN GOES OUTSIDE

Andrea Bandoni, Julia Masagão, Vapor 324, Marcos L. Rosa, ConstructLab

"As architects working together with the community, we recognised the urgent demands of the locals but also noticed we could think beyond what was expected from our work. To meet what was requested by locals and at the same time project the future of the initiative, we made a plan containing five layers. The point here is to activate a mindset that encourages new perspectives and interpretations of an urban area with the potential to activate urban life. By extending itself beyond its current limits, we imagine that the urban space in question can become a kind of "hub" in the context in which it is placed. The garden can "go out" to its neighbourhood in a way that the mobile kitchen can move around with different functions: as a cart to sell tapioca (suggested by Dona Sebastiana, a current worker of the garden), an alternative pharmacy, or a stand to sell vegetables or foods prepared with produce from the garden. On a larger scale, we imagine that the example of all gardens managed by "Cities Without Hunger" can contaminate the entire city, identifying areas of underused infrastructure to convert into productive spaces in every way: economically, socially, and creatively."

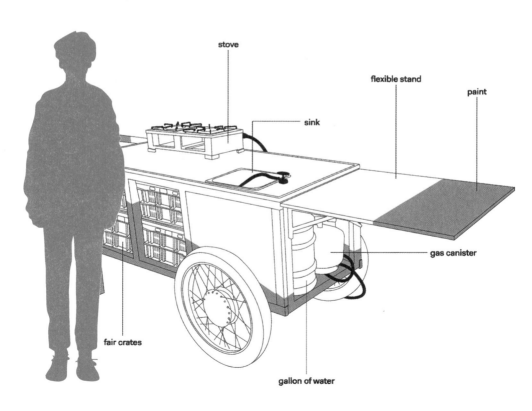

stove

flexible stand

paint

sink

fair crates

gallon of water

gas canister

THE EXQUISITE TRICICOL

Office of Urban Play

"In Mexico City, vendors blanket the city with a vast, informal, mobile market that crisscrosses Mexico City's sharply segregated communities. Exquisite Triciclo infiltrates these divided communities by appropriating the idiosyncratic cargo tricycle and hacking into the ambulantes' roaming sales network. Rather than selling tamales or drinking water, it turns this tool of commerce into a mobile stage, a public easel. Inspired by the surrealist parlour game of creating "exquisite corpses," the Triciclo endorses co-creation as a way to know thy neighbour. It makes stops outside schools, cantinas, tortillerias, eateries, and parks as well as locations unique to the area—courthouses, hospitals, universities—making no distinction between young or old, residents or passers-by. Its recorded merolico beckons all to come play and create. Equipped for collaborative creation in a variety of media—written, spoken, sculpted, recorded—the Triciclo plays out the personal, social, and cultural anxieties of the users it gathers by allowing uncensored and unguided communication.

Exquisite Triciclo is outfitted with GPS, a Go-Pro camera and a "Smart Pen", registering contrasting aesthetic and idiomatic differences pertaining to the residents of each neighbourhood. These devices keep a navigable digital record, as well as a tangible physical one, to be exhibited. The Triciclo's added technology is powered through its peddling thanks to a generator installed on the rear wheel. The tricycles of Mexico City are personal machines, pimped and decorated by their owners to attract attention. Exquisite Triciclo reflects its spirit in its making by gathering the knowledge and input of a diverse group of designers, fabricators, and community members to create a ludic instrument from creation through to use."

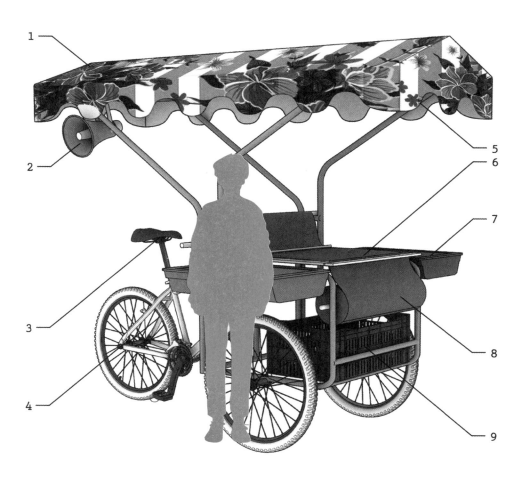

1. Sunshade
2. Megaphone
   (for merolico)
3. GPS Recording
4. Power Generator

5. GoPro camera(beneath canopy) recording activity surface
6. Activity surface (drawing, writing, recording, sculpting)

7. Activity supply bin (demountable)
8. Paper roll (demountable)
9. Large storage bin

GARDEN ARCHIPELAGO ROLLWAGEN

Atelier Fanelsa

"The project 'Garden Archipelago' investigates the latitudes for establishing modifications in public space in a seemingly fixed and unchangeable setting. Sonnenallee is one of Berlin's major traffic thoroughfares, cutting through the dense and lively area of Neukölln. The initial process started by asking for the possibility to physically modify and augment characteristic street furniture and vegetation, with minimal required effort and as an alternative to large-scale planning aiming to change the public setting as a whole. The project resulted in five micro-interventions in/through which different strategies were applied: repair work and modifications were made to existing street furniture elements; reproducible fences were constructed to allow for tree-pit gardening; traditional stone gardening techniques were adopted and a spice garden was built in the central reservation between traffic lanes, later cared for by two neighbouring barbershops. The activities all focused on the small green spaces, scattered down the center of Sonnenallee, as well as on the tree pits along the sidewalks. While following official regulations to the best possible extent, the project team aimed to test the possibilities of self-initiated gardening projects.The activities were conducted in close cooperation with local residents, interested in supporting and sustaining the activities themselves. To physically consolidate the activities a Rollwagen was built, comprised of a metal wheelbarrow base with a wooden frame built on top. The carriage used parts of a pushcart and contained plastic euro-boxes, typically used by the local greengrocers in the area. The vehicle not only allowed for the transportation of the tools and materials necessary for the interventions, it also served as a visible sign, a gathering spot for participants, and a conversation starter to engage with passers-by."

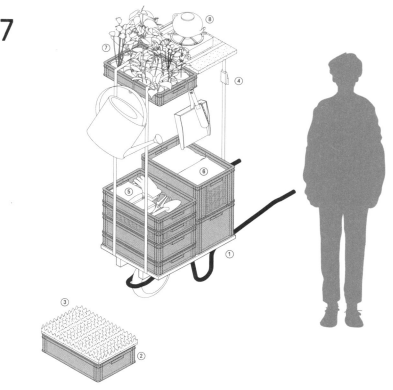

Image courtesy: Nikolas Fanelsa

100 BIKECROPOLIS

PINKCLOUD.DK

"Designed as a kit-of-parts, Bikecropolis builds upon the everyday pleasures of moving around the city. Momentarily, it focuses the disparate voices into concentrated spaces of speech and performance. Each cargo bike is paired with a customised trailer unit that contains all the parts necessary to set up the space, as well as outdoor furnishings. The design is easy to set up. First, a set of eight prefabricated steel poles are connected to form a circular "shower rod" that holds up a PVC curtain. The fully-connected ring is then hoisted to a height of nine feet with a telescopic tube built into the cargo bike. Tension cables are tied to four quadrants of the circle and the top of the telescopic tube to provide stability. The final result is an instant pavilion large enough to fit fifteen people. Hackable and scalable, more than one bike can be parked next to one another and combined to form an even larger space. Space is valued and created based on the sheer number of participating bikes: the more the bigger! Once the bike enclosures have been set up, a set of outdoor furnishings can be arranged adjacent to the pavilions. This furniture is DIY and modular, designed to accommodate seating, shelving, as well as tables. Its versatility can accommodate a variety of programming from performances, to pop-up shops, to block parties."

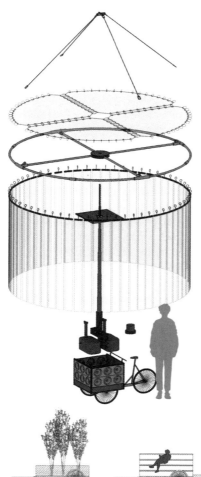

"A screen addiction epidemic plagues my city. As purveyors of endless information, screens feed us stories to inspire, to delude, to educate, to reassure, to agitate, to anger, and to entertain. Anything can be made available at our fingertips. We believe in individuality, equality, and all-you-can-eat freedom. I have my own story, and I have the right to tell it to the world. And now, more than ever, my voice can be heard. I can choose to see the wonders and the terrors across the globe, or I can stay within the comforts of my backyard. I can share my ideas with people I would have never known, and I can be empowered with all this information. I can see your stories, what you are eating, buying, doing.

Each individual constructs their own reality, but that reality is always a function of everyone else's. Inside this system, screens give us our fix of stories to consume. Collectively, we allow invisible hands to guide us in creating our stories, which in turn become realities of our society. But the voice that's heard is the voice that shouts the loudest. So, in any system, it becomes a means to (re)distribute power. This Co-machine is a manifestation of the stories we are feeding ourselves in a system that consumes us."

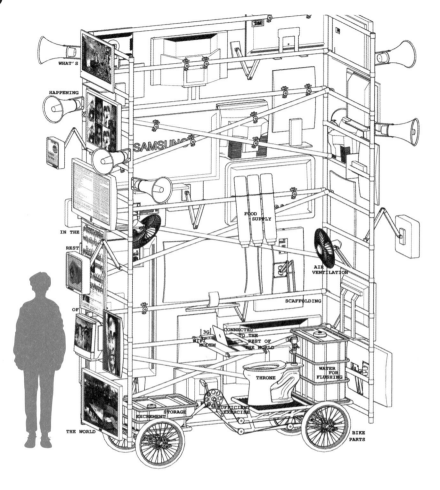

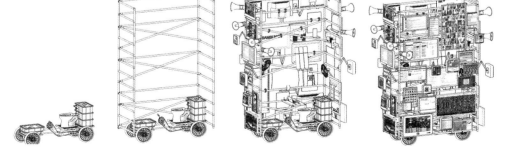

TROLLEY SOUND SYSTEM

Kaegh Allen

"The only good system is a sound system."

"This Co-machine was composed of a leisure battery from a hardware store, a simple and inexpensive car amp from the internet, and two old speakers from a home stereo system. This was all ratchet-strapped to an abandoned shopping trolley and elegantly decorated. The sound system was born from a long obsession with sound system culture and finally conjured up by the need for a cheap, quick, and movable system to lead a parade. But it soon became valuable for many other situations, from impromptu forest fires to a gathering point for protests, or simply to roll into house parties and energise situations. The system was implemented in Oxford, England. It was used as a centrepiece for a graduation parade, for forest fire backing music, and for gathering momentum during the 2010 student protests over raised university tuition fees. The system simply acted as a point of focus or momentary disruption and really highlighted to us that people only need a little help to loosen up and step away from a routine way of thinking and acting. The humble sound system is one of the simplest and most directly effective Co-machines. It was very modest and went through various manifestations; the battery had to be charged daily and was often impounded by police. The cheap amp blew once and had to be replaced for an upgraded version and we also added more second hand speakers, an electricity converter, lights, lasers, and hats to the very rudimentary but reliable and robust portable sound source. The project provides a valuable lesson in building for action, triggering many smiles and also many frowns, but mostly, it left a lot of happy memories. It is both easy to make and difficult not to enjoy."

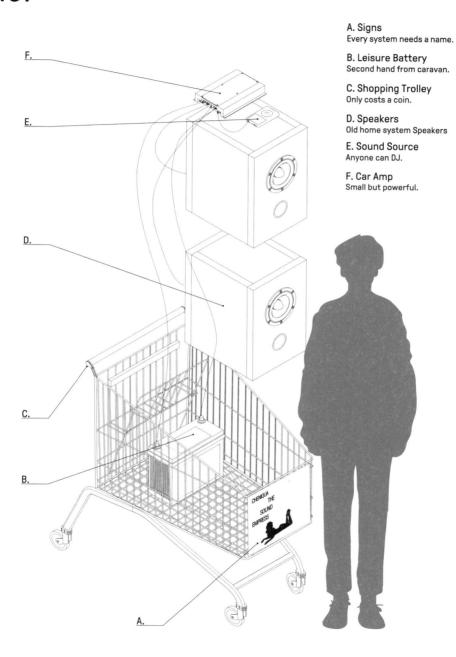

A. Signs
Every system needs a name.

B. Leisure Battery
Second hand from caravan.

C. Shopping Trolley
Only costs a coin.

D. Speakers
Old home system Speakers

E. Sound Source
Anyone can DJ.

F. Car Amp
Small but powerful.

F.

E.

D.

C.

B.

A.

CHEMOUA THE SOUND EMPRESS

108 FRAU FIBER AND THE BICYCLE-POWERED SEWING FACTORY

Carole Frances Lung

The Collaborative Bicycle-Powered Sewing Factory was conceived by Frau Fiber, a 21st-century textile activist whose actions do not easily come together into a systematic ideology. Her works expound and expand upon a single argument over a sequence of works and actions that span fast-fashion, revolution, the nature of honourably paid garment and textile labour, and the faculties of thought and judgment on the alternatives to capitalism as it relates to Fast-Fashion. The Collaborative Bicycle-Powered Sewing Factory reveal the collaborative aspects of apparel piecework and its ability to help create social bonds. These works are firmly connected to historical instances of organised labour and are a vehicle to think about self-sufficiency, self-empowerment, communal experience, and happiness in work, as well as a tool for fighting poverty and oppression. The machine intentionally has a direct link to the power of the peddler and no garment can be produced without their participation.

Image courtesy: Carole Frances Lung

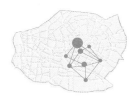

112 CHICKS ON SPEED

Stefanie Rittler and Jan Bernstein

"Nowadays we are consuming chicken as a product. So isn't it necessary to sharpen our awareness towards the food we are consuming and question the industrialisation of living creatures? In Germany alone, 97 million chickens are held in cages for meat production. 77% of these chickens are living in production environments with more than 50,000 animals. 39 million are held for egg production. In the past, a normal chicken laid 120 eggs per year, now it produces more than double that. These chickens only live for about one year before they are used for the meat industry. 48 million young male chickens get shredded alive directly after their birth. Space-wise, these chickens have 550cm^2 of living space, less than a DIN A4 sheet, or smaller than the size of this book when unfolded. Therefore one shopping cart fits 4.3 chickens. With a critical eye, this installation shows the discrepancy between the perception of these animals as creatures as opposed to a consumable product."

113

A. Folding roof
B. Window
C. Wheels
D. Chicken ladder & entrance
E. Walking chicken
F. Shopping cart

A.

B.

D.

C.

E.

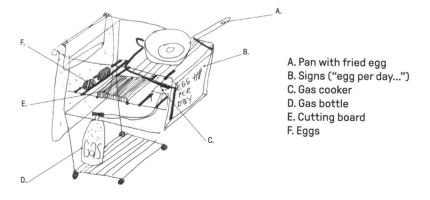

A.

F.

B.

E.

C.

D.

A. Pan with fried egg
B. Signs ("egg per day...")
C. Gas cooker
D. Gas bottle
E. Cutting board
F. Eggs

114 UNIDENTIFIED DRAWING OBJECT

Karin Blomgren & Joel Kerner

"Rather than being a conventional exhibition in a white room populated with pristine art, The Commons exhibition, as part of the 2015 Hardbakka Ruins Project in Bergen, Norway, sought to bring art out into the streets of the Mølenpris neighbourhood and engage the public through playful interventions. Most of the works produced for the exhibition were made from found and discarded materials in Bergen. The form of UDO's shell was inspired by the concrete barriers scattered around Mølenpris, while its handle drew inspiration from the many sailboats lining the water's edge. UDO invited people to hop on, ride it, do donuts, and see what was left behind. Lines were drawn by the playful apparatus, becoming the spatial residue of its journeys. During the course of the exhibition, people rode UDO to get to the various art pieces dispersed throughout the neighbourhood. The traces that were left behind by UDO acted as ephemeral way-finding, tying together the collective projects of the exhibition, and leading people towards their locations. The lines consisted of a mixture of clay powder and sawdust created from the production of all the exhibition pieces."

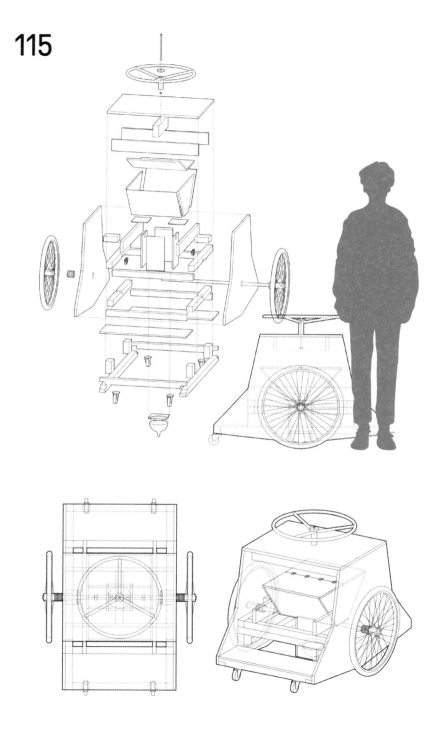

Image courtesy: Karin Blomgren and Joel Kerner

EXCHANGE MACHINE

Rachel Peachey & Paul Mosig

"The role of the Exchange Machine is to provoke people to think about how value is manufactured. This would occur through co-operative public interaction with friends or strangers while making an exchange. The machine asks you to place an object in it that isn't needed or wanted anymore so that you may receive something new without seeing what this new thing is beforehand. Once you have placed something in the machine you need two people to turn the wheels of the machine to reveal the new object. Although the machine is not complex, it opens up many interesting possibilities. Are you happy with the exchange in value between objects? Do you feel better or worse off and why? Why do some objects have so much more value than others? What gives them their value? Do you share the new object with the person who helped turn the other wheel? If it is not possible to share, how do you decide who keeps the object? How much value was there in the other person's help or does the value lie in the object alone? Are you willing to ask a stranger for help? What are you willing to give the object away for? Is the fun of the experience enough reward?

The exchange machine would be set up to operate in a public space like a park or local square, which is adjacent to a dense area of commercial activity including banks and shops. In this setting, the contrast between different ways of attributing value could be clearly felt. The portability of the machine would also mean that it could be set up in a variety of settings. It would be interesting to observe what type of objects are exchanged in different demographic areas, whether the objects tend towards traditionally high or low value items over time, and whether or not the exchanges change in regards to seasonality, time of day, and the length of time the machine is positioned somewhere."

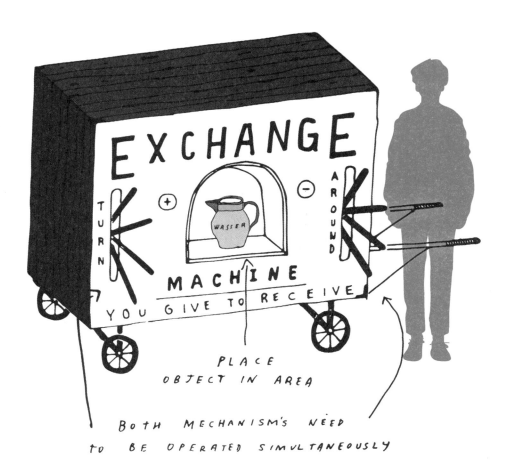

Image courtesy: Rachel Peachy & Paul Mosig

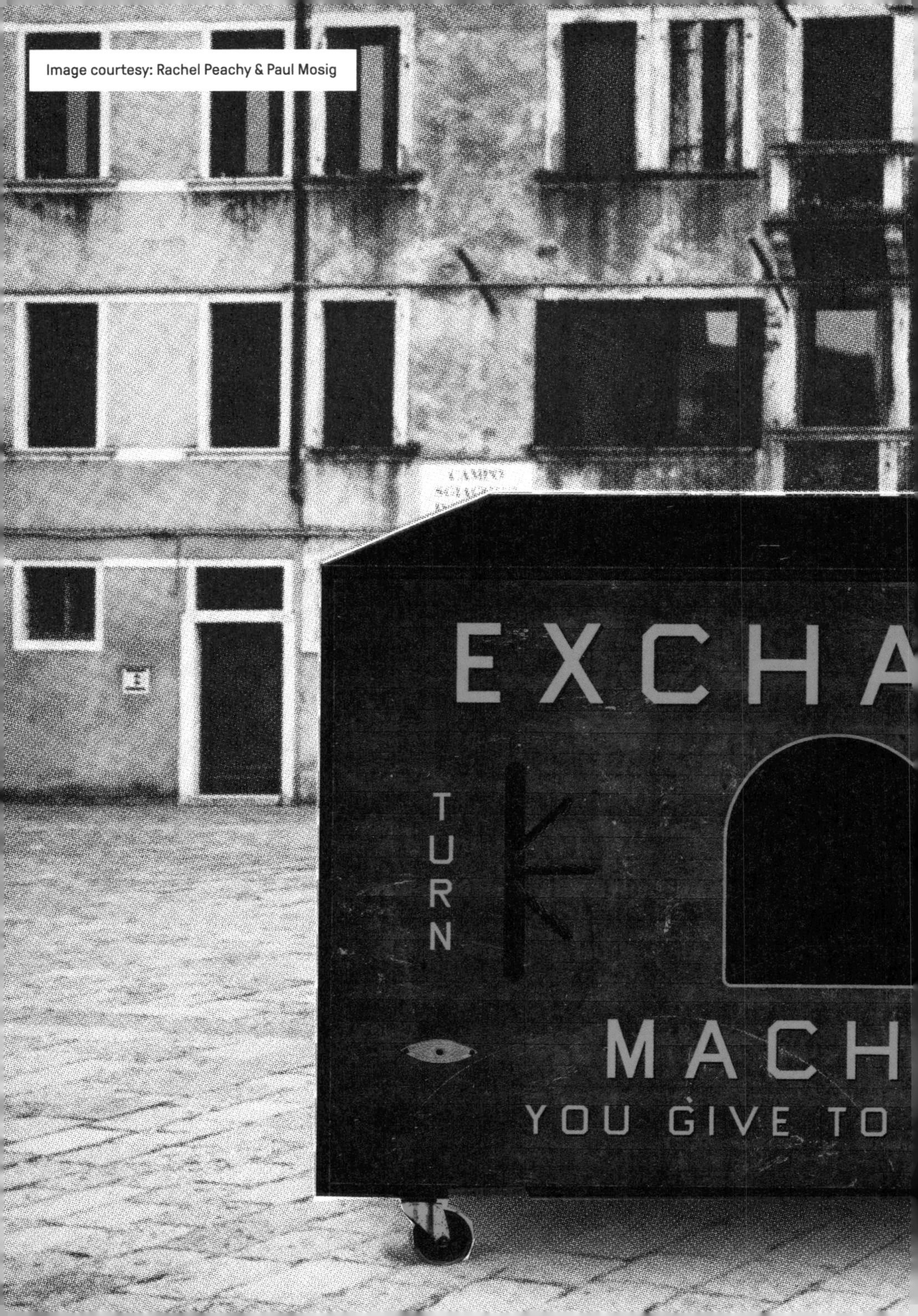

122 MOBILE RESEARCH VEHICLE

Realworld Laboratory for Sustainable Mobility Culture

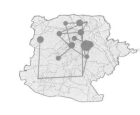

"Laboratories are for experiments. In a Realworld Laboratory, the experiments take place in an actual (spatial) environment to explore what effects new ideas can bring about and to examine how these influence a range of ecological, technical, and social boundary conditions. As such, the Realworld Laboratory for a Sustainable Mobility Culture invites the people of Stuttgart to tackle the challenges of urban mobility and try out new possible solutions in the form of Realworld Experiments. The Realworld Laboratory's Mobile Research Vehicle acts as a visible marker of an experiment in public space and serves as a tool for temporary placemaking. Unfolding minimal furniture and research material, it invites passers-by into a dialogue with the research of the Realworld Laboratory. It is based on a XYZ cargo trike (by N55 and Till Wolfer). Three of these vehicles have been built by a local cargo bike initiative 'Lastenrad Stuttgart' with Open Source construction manuals and have been made available as urban commons. The Mobile Research Vehicle enables the Realworld Laboratory's researchers and collaborators to undertake in situ research and experiential learning through transformative action, for example by riding with the Critical Mass and discussing the state of cycling in Stuttgart with cycling activists."

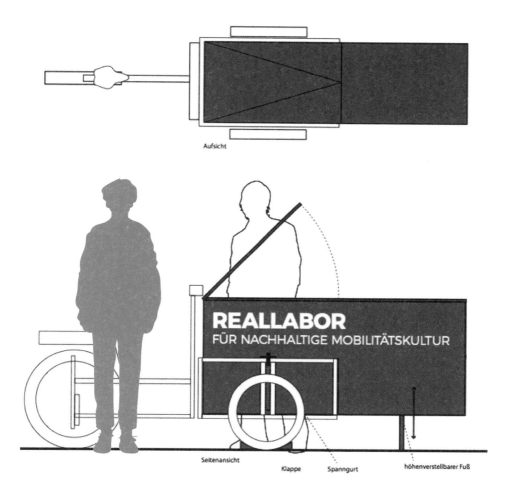

Aufsicht

REALLABOR
FÜR NACHHALTIGE MOBILITÄTSKULTUR

Seitenansicht

Klappe   Spanngurt   höhenverstellbarer Fuß

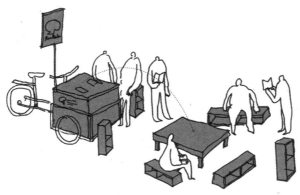

124 COCOOK MATADERO

Íñigo Cornago & Claudia Sánchez

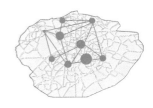

"Cocook is defined as a collaborative urban cooking project working on three levels: the collective design and construction of urban kitchen prototypes; the organisation of public events in which participants cook and eat together; and the exchange of everyday knowledge on these issues. The [Re] BUILDING THE CITY project is a reaction to the way public space has been designed in new European neighbourhoods built over the past decades. In these areas, the tendency has been to sell and reproduce a specific image of the city, following the market economy's principles and pace, while ignoring the dynamics, social fabric, and rituals that give sense to them and have built the city historically. The aim of the project is to revive the idea that public space is also the place to create, build, enjoy, and share. THE [open] EVENT IS THE [public] SPACE; The event is considered on the same level as the space. We see spaces such as the kitchen and the workshop as spaces of collective creativity, experimentation and mutual learning. Cocook proposes to bring them out of their usually enclosed domestic and professional environments into the public realm. Through relational and amateur collaboration, and thanks to the exposure and diversity of public space, the exchange and enjoyment grows exponentially. THE PRODUCTION [and communication] OF SPACE; For Cocook, contingency, assembly, and collage are key aspects. The urban kitchen prototypes are built using found, loaned, or donated materials. Likewise, the food is cooked based on the ingredients brought and gathered by the participants as well as their knowledge. As a result, the tools used to develop, document and communicate the project, such as recipes, DIY Kits or manuals, enable their partial adaptation and combination to be implemented in other contexts."

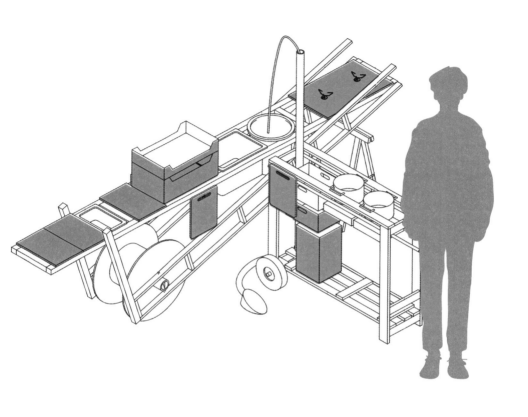

126 BASTIAN DER STADT:SYMBIONT

Guerilla Architects

"Bastian der Stadt:Symbiont—a co-working space inside a caravan—is a guideline for the autonomous creation of a working space in the city. Rental prices for studio spaces are rising uncontrolled, the creative industries face increasingly unstable working conditions, flexible working models, short-term contracts and precarious payments. Despite this, or maybe because of this, many creatives are dreaming of autonomy. Without a stable income it is often impossible to rent an office space for the long term. We need to explore new fields of action: future architecture means city-hacking. We understand the city as an existing network of diverse infrastructures that everyone can use. Working "between the lines" of laws and parking regulations, we developed a guide for central, long-lasting, and cost-efficient working spaces. Free resources—wi-fi, public toilets, canteens—complete the independent, always on-site, long-term, and cheap architecture office and connect the small-scale working space to the large-scale city. The Stadt:Symbiont promotes a social exchange as a visible institution and meeting place for residents and passers-by. This exchange of thoughts, ideas and knowledge is the basis for our work. Always in movement, the architect's workspace and field of work merge on site."

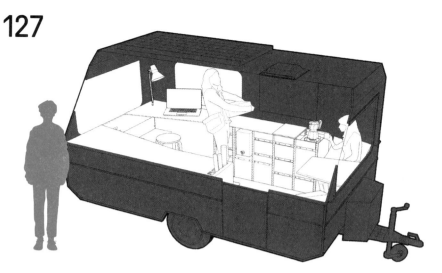

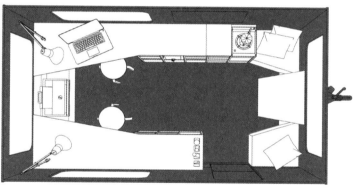

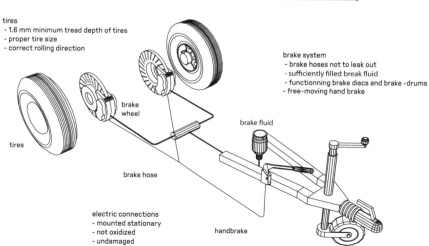

tires
- 1.6 mm minimum tread depth of tires
- proper tire size
- correct rolling direction

brake system
- brake hoses not to leak out
- sufficiently filled break fluid
- functionning brake discs and brake -drums
- free-moving hand brake

tires

brake wheel

brake fluid

brake hose

electric connections
- mounted stationary
- not oxidized
- undamaged

handbrake

128 CREATION STATION

Philipp von Hase

"A creation is achieved through the act of making or producing. A station refers to a base that is equipped for research, service, and work. The Creation Station is a giant mobile toolbox equipped with basic hand tools. It is a free and open workspace that acts as a platform for prototyping, building, inventing, or fixing stuff locally and publicly. The platform provides for workshops and do-it-yourself activities within the commons. It activates urban space and facilitates maker culture: mainly involving learning practical skills and applying them creatively. The Creation Station also provides space for parking a cargo bike or storing materials. It is entirely open access. All the hand tools are hooked to the station with long metal wires. Two awnings above provide shelter from rain and sun. The station is made of steel frames and water-resistant plywood. For levelling and lifting, it has integrated car jacks in each corner, combined with cargo wheels that can be flipped out for transport. The Creation Station is an open access space and open source project. The material, cutting lists, and the overall budget for production of such a station are available on the Creation Station blog."

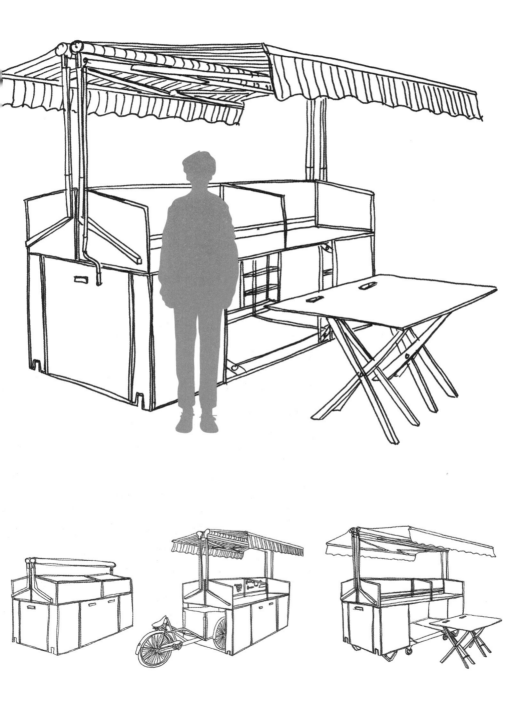

Office for Political Innovation

"In Madrid, contemporary art centres and other large cultural institutions tend to concentrate along the axis that joins Avenida de América with Legazpi Square, aligned with the city center. In contrast, small music, theatre, or poetry groups are, for the most part, evenly scattered throughout the capital's extensive territory. Although these small groups culturally stimulate the local contexts in which their activities develop individually, considered as a collective, they constitute the biggest cultural infrastructure in the city. This produces a large impact in terms of cultural promotion and debate activities. Matadero Madrid, a former slaughterhouse turned cultural institution, is described as a 'public space for contemporary culture, with views on the river'. The aim of our project is to endow it with the necessary material devices and institutional protocols to prompt a connection between the aforementioned models of intervention in the cultural field. This activates their potential as a broader collective network. To achieve this, the scheme proposes equipping the open spaces of the old abattoir with varied types of large-span mobile structures with sound-amplifying systems, stage lighting, and audiovisual projection systems in combination with sliding stands, that may serve as auxiliary structures for public performances. The use of these facilities is organised following the conventions of the local municipal tennis courts, which are booked by the hour. The structure's materials are based on the idea of an odd assemblage of inexpensive elements: irrigation systems, polythene fabric from the greenhouses of the Spanish province of Almería, or cheap plastic chairs. It is a composite of ready-mades, using existing technologies in ways that differ from their original intent. It is a technological re-appropriation process, which the office relates to the possibility of queer uses of available systems."

escaravox

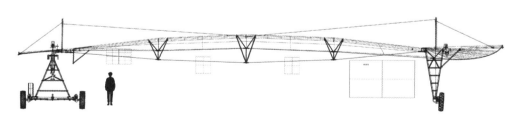

Office for Political Innovation /
Andrés Jaque

Escaravox
Madrid, Spain

Solid Operation

"Matroshka Street Furniture is a mobile installation which aims for the playful transformation of public spaces into places of cooperation. This simple design is open to interpretation and engages people of all ages in temporary placemaking strategies. Without predefining the function of its pieces, a group can arrange and rearrange the boxes according to its needs and include the context of the urban space and play. Each time a new constellation is tested, a new space is created. Matroshka Street Furniture derives its name from the Russian nested dolls, called "Matryoshka". The basic idea is to maximise the amount of pieces while minimising storage space. All pieces can be stacked inside one big box, which itself gets attached to a platform on wheels. This way, it can easily be transported by foot or even taken on public transport. The boxes, from the smallest to the biggest, have been designed to be stacked inside and on top of each other or lie on their sides. It is up to the people using them to get creative, interpret their uses and create new situations together. The first prototype is made out of 8mm beech plywood, which we connected through dowels and painted with clear sealant. Depending on the group's building skills, available tools and time, easier connection-methods like screws can be used as well. Also, the choice of material can vary but most important for the design is that you build with precision or leave more play so that the boxes can be stacked. Have fun!"

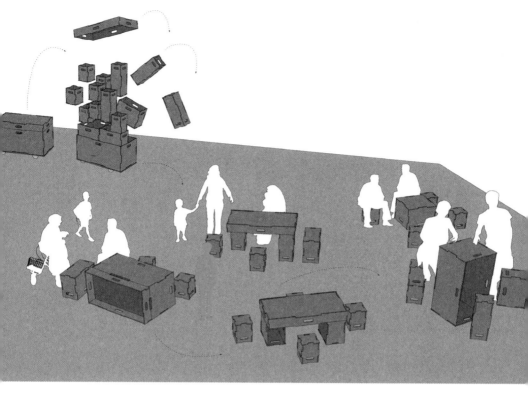

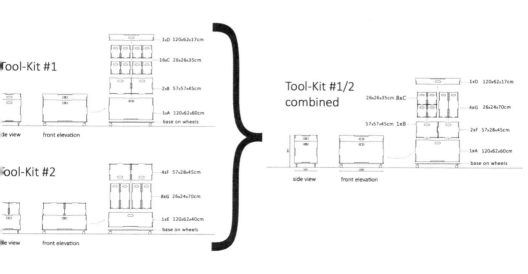

Tool-Kit #1

side view   front elevation

1xD 120x62x17cm
16xC 26x26x35cm
2xB 57x57x45cm
1xA 120x62x60cm
base on wheels

Tool-Kit #2

side view   front elevation

4xF 57x28x45cm
8xG 26x24x70cm
1xE 120x62x40cm
base on wheels

Tool-Kit #1/2
combined

side view   front elevation

1xD 120x62x17cm
26x26x35cm 8xC
4xG 26x24x70cm
57x57x45cm 1xB
2xF 57x28x45cm
1xA 120x62x60cm
base on wheels

136 PRECIOUS PLASTIC

Dave Hakkens

"Annually, we produce unimaginable quantities of plastic. Last year, we produced 311 million tons, but less than 10% of this plastic gets recycled. Most of it will end up in the wrong place, such as landfills or oceans, eventually to be consumed by wildlife. Although this damages our ecosystem Big Plastic prefers to work with new plastic, as recycled plastic might slow down production or damage machines. Currently people lack machines to start recycling plastic themselves. Precious Plastic has developed machines that enable people to start recycling plastic. The machines are specifically developed using universal materials and basic tools that are available all over the world. The blueprints, a series of detailed instruction videos, and the download-kit, are shared open source online. This is all the basic information people need to build their own machines and start a little plastic factory—anywhere in the world—and set up small-scale production to create valuable things. Acting as a craftsman of plastic, they can make products, raw material, set up a production site, clean up their neighbourhood, and start their own business. We share all the information for people to start their own little plastic factory, for free online. For this to have an impact, we need to make sure people actually know this information exists. We need help to spread this information around the globe and let people know they can now start to work with plastic. Once the information is spread, the recycling begins!"

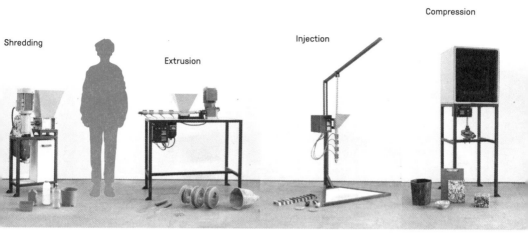

Shredding

Extrusion

Injection

Compression

Some of the products created from reused plastic

Image courtesy: Precious Plastic

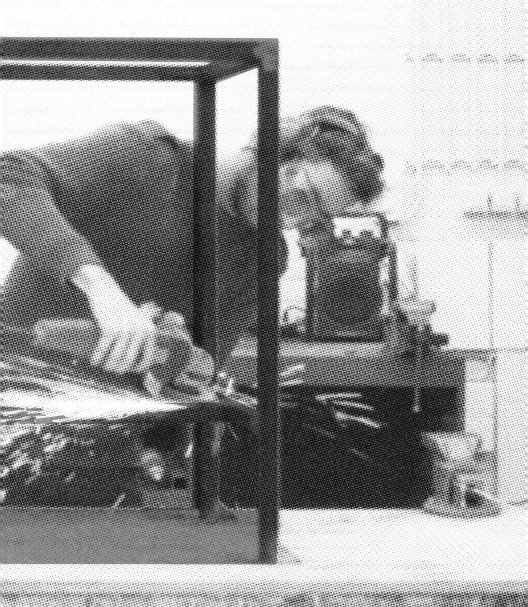

140 MOBILE CO.MPOSTER

Leonard Daisuke Yui & Sahoko Yui

"Can composting engage the public realm? How is it relevant today? Composting has long been the interest of farmers, environmentalists, and scientists, but more notably it was an act of everyday life. Industrialisation, concerns of public health, and rapid urban development transformed the relationship with food waste from personal engagement to large-scale productions. There is a growing need to re-engage composting as a public event and bring agency to the food waste process. The need to stimulate renewal and curiosity centres around a duty to make more visible and tangible the ecological cycle of waste. Transitioning cities like Providence, Rhode Island and depressed neighbourhoods like the Tenderloin District in San Francisco offer opportunities to rethink the nature of cities as they adapt to social, environmental, and economic changes. Our proposal is an ecological machine that interactively consumes our food waste and generates beneficial relationships with beings around it. The biodigester facilitates the anaerobic composting process of organic material and converts it into biogas and inorganic fertiliser. The heat byproduct produced from the composting process generates microclimatic change by warming the surrounding temperature and extending the planting season and providing extra warmth on cold nights. In addition, the Co-machine features edible habitats for human and non-human species by linking food production through community gardens, green roofs, and park spaces to mobilise nourishment and habitation beyond traditional urban infrastructures. Covertly, sensors on the machine coordinate and learn movements like self-driving vehicles. They learn patterns in public spaces and behaviour, so the machine can respond accordingly."

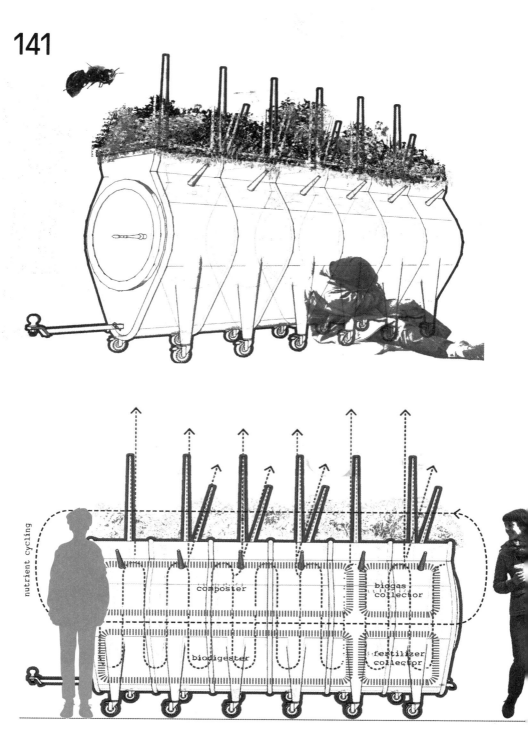

composter

biogas collector

biodigester

fertilizer collector

nutrient cycling

Alexander v. Lenthe

"The 100m Apparatus consists of the following: a distance meter to measure 100m of a public street to be occupied by a racetrack; two barriers, to block the way; water; chalk, to mark the start and the finish line; medals and a podium to award to the runners. It is a device for militant pedestrians that aims to fight traffic, extend the boundaries of pedestrian territory, and continue the battle of People vs. Cars as a means to reclaim the streets and make Henry Ford history. Urbanists proclaim a shift towards a pedestrian-friendly city, but "reduced traffic areas" are not the answer. The 100m Apparatus will trigger a pedestrian movement, in the vein of the Critical Mass for the cyclist. Figures in different cultural contexts have understood the symbolic potential of running: Forrest Gump, Lola, Mark Zuckerberg, Joschka Fischer, Tommie Smith and John Carlos, Raymond Belle.

The 100m Apparatus sees running as an act of liberation.

The 100m Apparatus is not one of a kind.

It will be copied and altered. It will grow in size and its use will vary over time. But it will always stay a tool for re-appropriation. We will start to see the 100m Apparatus in small neighbourhoods, but soon it will be in action on Karl-Marx-Allee, on Champs-Élysées, and Route 66."

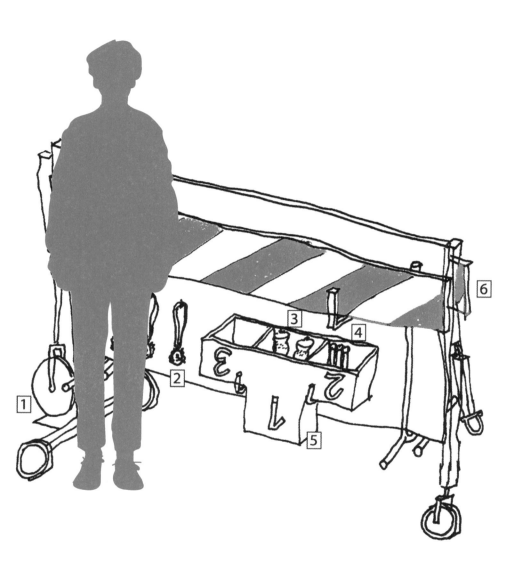

1. Distance Meter
2. Medals
3. Water
4. Chalk
5. Podiums
6. Barriers

Image courtesy: Alexander v. Lenthe

Andrea Orving

"Since a large part of public space revolves around the transportation and storage of cars, the Sleeping Armour addresses this hierarchy and lifestyle. The demand for more ecologically and socially-sound means of transportation has grown in urgency. By presenting an alternative use of public space, which is as necessary as the need for transportation, the Sleeping Armour opens up the dialogue toward prevalent concerns in the city regarding mobility and densification. This low-income, non-site-bound alternative provokes discussion concerning hierarchies, gentrification, and segregation. Basically: who is welcome where? The wagon induces discussion concerning how we can create more heterogeneous neighbourhoods and an open and accessible city. The idea is to exploit public or semi-public facilities such as boat clubs, water posts, public toilets, and swimming facilities. Given the mobile and temporary nature of the vehicle, it can inhabit spaces otherwise not suited for temporary housing due to, for example, the absence of a building permit. This includes land about to be transformed or built upon, non-spaces and temporarily unused land, and parking lots or parking house rooftops. It's an opportunity to have overlapping programming of a city and maximised use of space. Housing meets different needs for different people at different times. The need for a large, static home is not always a priority. While for a privileged few, housing must satisfy the desperate need for an ocean view, for others, just having shelter matters. Creating the latter alternative to the existing housing market presents a range of alternative ways of living. The aim is not to marginalise the vulnerable individuals seeking shelter. Instead, we can open up our minds towards flexible housing solutions and view all attempts as symbols of a more generous society with new alternatives and horizons."

147

A. Mail Drop
B. Built-in Planters
C. Double Doors
D. Railing
E. Bed
F. Shell
G. Freshwater Tank
H. Graywater Tank
I. Camera Obscura
   Peephole
J. Motor

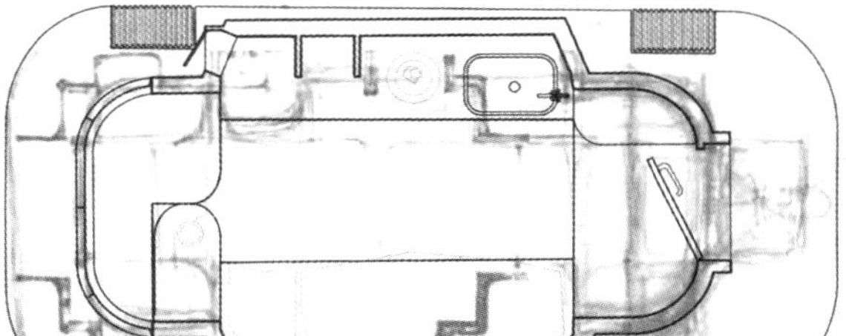

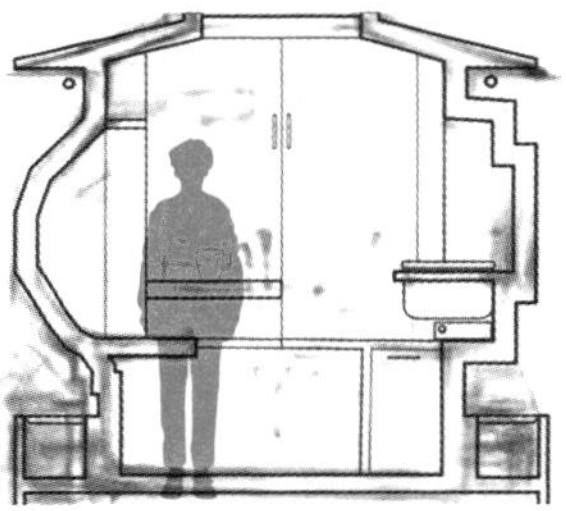

A.

B.

C.

G.

H.

D.

E.

F.

I.

J.

148 MOBILE RECONFIGURABLE POLYHEDRA

Interactive Architecture Lab / William Bondin, Ruairi Glynn, Francois Mangion

"MORPHs, short for Mobile Reconfigurable Polyhedra, are adaptive octahedral structures that can roll around public spaces and respond to their physical environment. Their intent is to provide a dynamic and playful environment for play areas within public parks, and to encourage young generations to engage with computational technology from an early age. Each robotic structure is composed of twelve actuated struts and can morph its geometry in order to be able to shift its center of gravity. This ability allows it to roll-over from one place to another autonomously. The octahedrons can be controlled wirelessly, and the onboard GPS module assists in defining a boundary for the robot to operate in. Alternatively, each machine can be programmed by squeezing the tactile joints at each end of the struts. These two modes of operation allow for a wider range of interactions to take place."

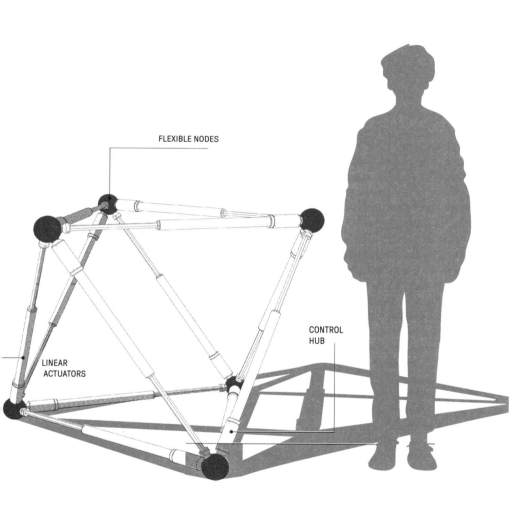

FLEXIBLE NODES

LINEAR
ACTUATORS

CONTROL
HUB

MOVEMENT

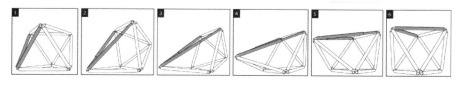

TRANSPARENT FOOTPRINTS OF INVISIBLE GIANTS MACHINE

Takehito Etani

"The Transparent Footprints of Invisible Giants Machine interrupts everyday routines on urban streets, replacing the myopic vision of modern daily life with micro/macro cosmic vision that connects the present to the remote past and distant future. The walking machines (stilts) will incorporate downward facing video cameras under each foot that record virtual video footprints. The cameras document and map various street surfaces such as concrete, asphalt, cobblestones, and lawns, thereby leaving footprints on the digital stratum of the 21st century. Another video camera placed above the head records the sky and an audio recorder with a stereo microphone records the urban soundscapes. Wearing these machines is a transformative experience, as the wearer becomes a gentle giant slowly and consciously treading the Earth with an eye to both heaven and earth. During the walking expedition, an online map will display the progress by GPS in real time. Following the expedition, the video footprints and the sky videos will be uploaded on the map. These video recordings will become video installations. The footprint video will be projected on the door, and the sky video projected on the ceiling. Simultaneous viewing of the projected images will mimic an invisible giant traveling through the vast space between the sky and earth. The backpack transforms into a mobile living machine: a functional living unit with a sleeping cot, tent, and a work desk to serve as a mobile base camp during longer treks."

151

a. Video camera : Sky
b. Microphone
c. Video Monitors
d. Rear View Mirror
e. Laptop + GPS

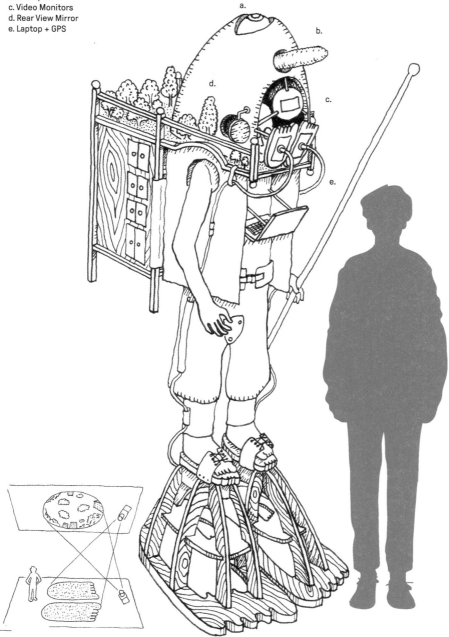

152 DANCE VEHICLE 01

Marcus Shaffer, Alex Bruce,
Kyle Brown, Will Bunk

"Dance Vehicle 01 is the result of an experimental collaboration in the fields of architecture and dance. The focus of the studio challenged our team to reexamine the increasingly overlooked and discarded social interactions that occur in public spaces. During the machine's deployment for an hour-long performance on Penn State University's campus, dancers walked, drove, rode, climbed, and jumped through the vehicle. The machine responds in tandem as a steel dance partner, thus revitalising public space through performance design. The vehicle dances, transferring human movement into a performance and enables dancers to experiment in a medium free of gravity or limitations of conventional dance space. Pedestrians and passers-by interact and experience the act of transportation and movement in new ways. The perforated panels on the vehicle's walking surface, negative spaces in the shape of smartphones, form viewports that encourage users to peer through and physically engage with the act of their own movement. By discouraging walking with your head down, the perforations frame moments and remind us how beautiful public spaces can be when free from the intrusion of electronics and social media. The vehicle is composed of two truss-framed wheels encasing a suspended triangular antiprism cage. The rotating cage creates an occupiable space for performers to hang, suspend, act, and react to the machine's rapidly changing movements. The vehicle is "driven" by performers walking in the outer rings, who can change its speed and orientation by walking forwards or backwards. The intricate construction of the rolling mechanism allows all three components to spin independently of one another."

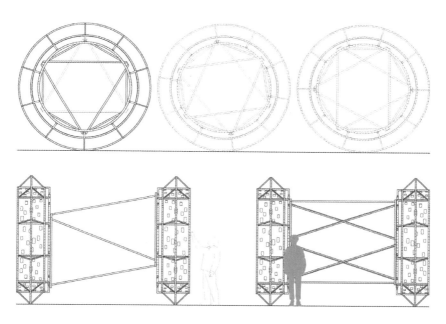

Image courtesy: Alex Bruce, Kyle Brown, Will Bunk, Marcus Shaffer

Ahmad S. Khouja

"The urban landscape is saturated with obtrusive monuments of real estate development and propagandised advertisements. These structures infringe upon the public domain so that little is left outside the reach of financial speculation. So severe is the situation that one day, one might be living next to a historic lighthouse that has served the public good for hundreds of years (i.e., the famous Manara neighbourhood lighthouse in Beirut, Lebanon) and the next, it is shut down so that luxury apartments may occupy its views and not be bothered by pesky navigational beams of light. But beams of light can be repositioned and these barren concrete walls can be instruments of counter-propaganda. In this capacity, The Nimble Lighthouse fills a void. Compact, mobile, and rechargeable, it is equipped to turn any city wall into an outdoor cinema. The protracting projector can display an image 5-15 meters away and roughly 2-5 meters above the ground. Also included is a short-wave radio transmitter capable of broadcasting signals within a 5 metre radius; receivable through any mobile phone device with radio function and a pair of headphones. No permit, no zoning, no problem…just mobile guerrilla cinema."

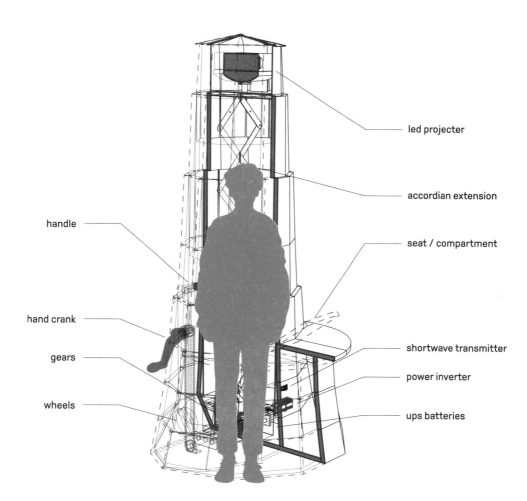

led projecter

accordian extension

handle

seat / compartment

hand crank

gears

shortwave transmitter

wheels

power inverter

ups batteries

Jason Vigneri-Beane

"The Mecha_A38 /// Dark_Invader is designed to be deployed in urban environments and, in particular, in Privately Owned Public Spaces (POPS) in New York City. POPS are a special category of urban space wherein developers are granted premiums on their investments in exchange for providing some surplus value for the city or accommodation to the citizenry, such as exterior green or paved space. These spaces can be welcome relief or frameworks for profound tensions across scales and legal boundaries. They can become lovely and accommodating urban oases or sites of oppression that came to the forefront of public consciousness during the Occupy Wall Street movement. The tensions seem to be steadily increasing as they become emphatically cleansed, secured, regulated, and policed. While one perhaps understands the complexities of the global city, one does not have to surrender to the lack of expression, sense of homogenisation, and feeling of paranoia that now sadly surrounds the idea of public space in some globalised cities. The Dark Invader is meant to engage, in its own small and optimistic way, with this evolving scenario. The Dark Invader would be deployed as a mobile, automated, and responsive architectural agent with micro-infrastructural capabilities. It can move about, deploy its drones, project its content, and provide its small services to the public as it navigates these double-edged urban scenarios of opportunity and constraint. It would be a kind of fellow-traveler that can comfort people with climate and water, connect people with networking and messaging technologies, and boost the voice of those who would like to relay a small message to a large collective."

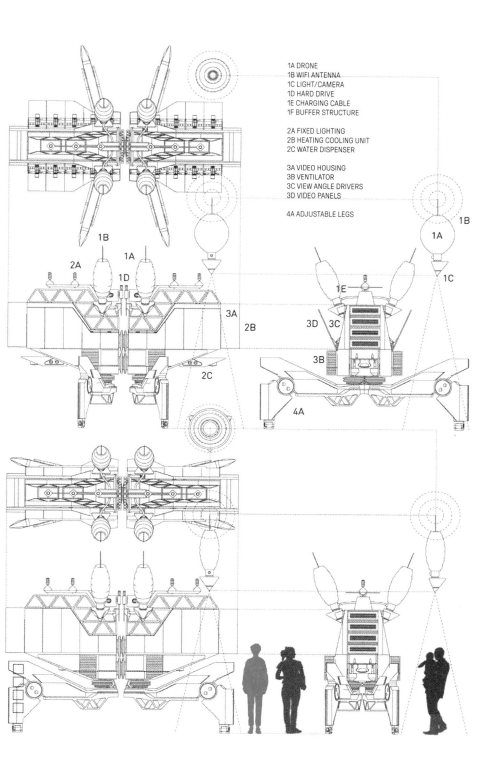

1A DRONE
1B WIFI ANTENNA
1C LIGHT/CAMERA
1D HARD DRIVE
1E CHARGING CABLE
1F BUFFER STRUCTURE

2A FIXED LIGHTING
2B HEATING COOLING UNIT
2C WATER DISPENSER

3A VIDEO HOUSING
3B VENTILATOR
3C VIEW ANGLE DRIVERS
3D VIDEO PANELS

4A ADJUSTABLE LEGS

160 A CHICKEN MEMORIAL

Tal Mor Sinay

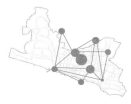

"The Chicken Memorial is subversive, informal, mobile, and parasitic to the public realm. It does not operate as one might imagine a machine would, and in that sense, it might seem dysfunctional. However, it has a clear function and mission: to question society's perceptions of commemoration and how the grieving process is operated in the public realm. It is a memorial for a real hen, raised in my house as a pet for approximately two years. Private memorials built by private people on public grounds, mostly on roadsides, are a well-known phenomenon in countries such as Israel and Australia. These objects usually commemorate war casualties or loved ones who died in traffic accidents. They have a distinctive visual character and a clear visual code, even though they are very different from one another. The act of placing such a private memorial could be seen as a violent act, whereby one takes control of public space, making its location and its very existence taboo. My Co-machine attempts to sneak its way into the pantheon of "informal memorials" to enjoy the privileges granted to such objects. It also examines the boundaries of the visual and functional rules of the memorialisation realm.

The Chicken Memorial was planned and designed to be portable. Its lightweight structure, its surrounding carrying handles, and its ability to tie itself to its surroundings support this portability. Furthermore, it is equipped with a solar light element with a light sensor that illuminates as it gets dark and makes it more independent. The light's shape was designed as a graphic icon, referring to the hen's footprint. It can be moved from one location to another, and thus it is constantly engaging and changing the public domain. Over a period of one month, it travelled around Israel and was placed in various public places ranging from countryside, urban landscape, and desert.

Solar Light element- designed as an icon referring to the hen's footprint.

Solar panel- allows for independent operation.

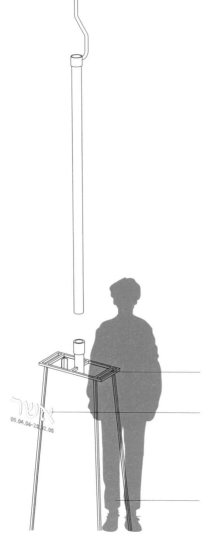

Top carying handles.

Hen's name (Asher) date of birth and death written in the most common font used in the memorialization practice in Israel.

The main body is constructed from a metal frame and sheets. It is light weight to enable easy transportation.

162 PARKING LOFT

Atelier Slant

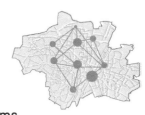

"The Parking Loft is our battlewagon. It reclaims the ground by occupying a parking space (the footprint of one car) to then transform it into a dwelling for two humans. This temporary and fluid occupation makes use of the public space, not to generate income but to establish alternative living situations that are accessible to everyone. The Parking Loft machine is a retrogressive machine. It belongs to a new generation of machines that rejects standardisation, alienation, automation, and high-technology—thus, it is non-modern. Behaving like a parasite, it can adapt to the context and benefit from the circumstances. It moves on wheels but also forms roots to expand to start a mutually-symbiotic relationship with the street. Made up of two interdependent core modules, which provide the minimum living space for the two inhabitants, the house can split and open up in many different ways. For instance, a wooden palette wall, armed with sharp spurs, becomes a terrace, a public stage, or a common door between the two core elements. Similarly, a plastic envelope folds in and out to provide shelter; multiple openings guarantee different degrees of interaction with the street, and a periscope on the roof blocks the light from the adjacent lamp post into the apartment. The Parking Loft is low-tech, low-budget, and made of junk! One machine is never like the other, as its components are sourced in the specific habitat where it settles and may vary according to different local circumstances. Its configuration is determined by the needs and the temporary uses that one makes of it. The Parking Loft supports diversity, not uniformity."

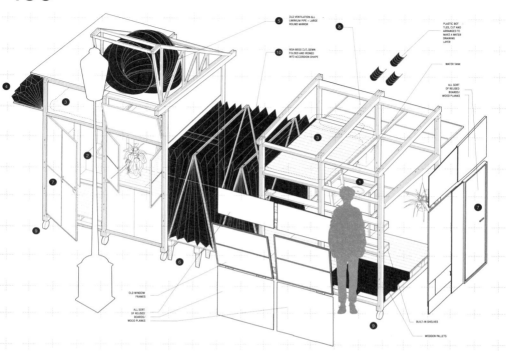

OLD VENTILATION ALL
LIMINIUM PIPE + LARGE
ROUND MIRROR

PLASTIC BOT
TLES, CUT AND
ARRANGED TO
MAKE A WATER
DRAINING
LAYER

RISA-BEGS CUT, SEWN
FOLDED AND IRONED
INTO ACCORDION SHAPE

WATER TANK

ALL SORT
OF REUSED
BOARDS/
WOOD PLANKS

OLD WINDOW
FRAMES

ALL SORT
OF REUSED
BOARDS/
WOOD PLANKS

BUILT-IN SHELVES

WOODEN PALLETS

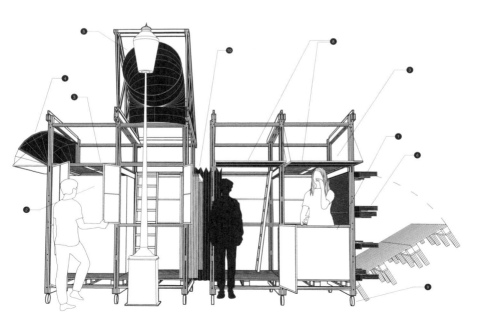

166 #OCCUPY PETITE CEINTURE: AN ARCHITECTURAL OPERATION

Atilla Ali Tasan

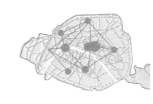

"Parks and squares, though publicly accessible, are not public property in the true sense. Public spaces in city centres are increasingly surveilled spaces with controlled and restricted access and therefore less spontaneous and creative. The occupation is an attempt to reclaim these territories. It is more than a way to manifest ideologies, it is an intervention that takes place in a pre-defined architectural realm. The occupiers create novel ways of using the public space and propose complex spatial engagements in the cityscape. This project explores the interaction, organisation, and the communication of the individuals within an emergent context and identifies possible areas for architectural legacy from these heterotopic places. Petite Ceinture is an abandoned rail track circling Paris, a no man's land between central Paris and the Périphérique. It is made of multiple units that travel along the abandoned rail track. This train convoy establishes the framework for a stigmergic space-making organisation. Each unit in the convoy serves as a fabrication hub and provides infrastructure for an insurgent construction scheme in post-industrial Paris.

A Machine for Occupation and the existing structures do not attempt to occupy the same functional space. But given that the train convoy is a transient architecture, always looking for a new station, the next place to plug-in, they create a dialogue to recognise this urban buffer zone. In this continuous material cast, it is essential to remember that the geometry is utilised, not produced. Occupying the interstitial space of urbanism, these assembled structures create a temporary condition for the community. The coupled occupier and park become a laboratory for future urban studies. The city is assimilated as a single modifiable substance that can be worked on and reconfigured to meet these needs. A new society is engendered by the form of this new 'suburb'."

onents

Plant Room

Extruder

Steel Foreworks

Anchor Points

Structural Pillar

Containment Unit

Retaining Wall Unit

Flatbed Train Car

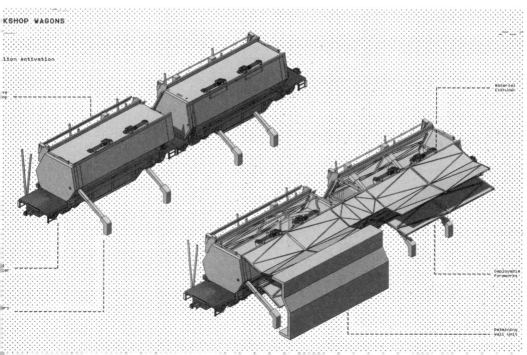

KSHOP WAGONS

lion Activation

Material
Extruder

Deployable
Foreworks

Retaining
Wall Unit

168 HORTUM MACHINA B

Interactive Architecture Lab /
William Victor Camilleri and Danilo
Sampaio

"As Hortum Machina B is only the first prototype of the research, it cannot manoeuvre itself around the city safely amongst people and vehicle traffic. Nonetheless, it has been closely tested on the streets of London, as well as in a park on a few occasions. Although it is not yet equipped with collision avoidance abilities, it carries a GPS that tracks its location as well as the distance it has travelled, meaning that the prototype is able to remain in safe areas if need be. Needless to say, the presence of a gigantic 3-metre sphere full of plants left people in awe. Although seemingly an imposing mechanical structure, passers-by still wanted to touch the plants and climb onto the geodesic sphere, while others opted to go for the instinctive selfie. Harnessing the collective intelligence of plant behaviour, the Hortum Machina B explores new forms of bio-cooperative interaction between people and nature, within the built environment. Its core of twelve garden modules, each carrying native British species on outwardly-extending linear actuators, allow the structure to become mobile by shifting its centre of gravity. Electro-physiological sensing of the state of individual plants collectively and democratically controls decision-making of the orientation of the structure and its mobility. In the current context of driverless cars, and many other forms of intelligent robotics beginning to cohabit our built environment, Hortum Machina B acts as a speculative urban cyber-gardener, moving around the city, repopulating its species by discovering suitable microclimates. The mobilisation of the plants' agency acts as a provocation, drawing attention to their very "living-ness" and our shared goal on Buckminster Fuller's Spaceship Earth: to find and build better places to live and thrive. With Hortum Machina B we hope that the playfulness of the garden robot invites everyone in to consider more deeply the needs of not just ourselves, but all the passengers of Spaceship Earth."

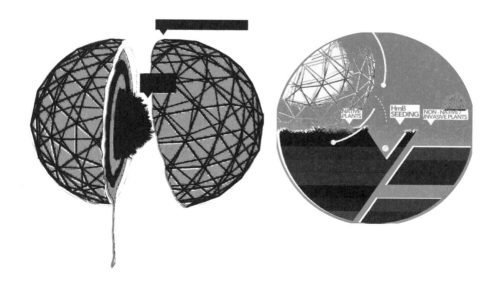

LINEAR ACTUATOR

ALUMINIUM CORE

SOLAR PANEL

GARDEN

WATER STORAGE

ACRYLIC PLANTING POT

STEEL CABLE

NATIVE PLANTS

HmB SEEDING

NON-NATIVE/ INVASIVE PLANTS

170 CONSTRUCTION DE L'ASSOCIATION

Julia Klauer

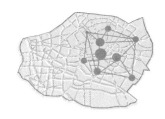

"Urban wastelands are among some of the most adaptive spaces in cities because they have no defined function and therefore processes can develop according to the particular environment. This spatial intervention with a modular dodecahedron intends to discover the potential of a wasteland. The dodecahedron consists of bike rims connected by cable ties, flexible in style and function depending on the urban context and user (designer). The modular dodecahedron construction and shape was inspired by Buckminster Fuller, a Comprehensive Anticipatory Design Scientist. I combined fascination with pure form and a pragmatic do-it-yourself approach: twelve old bike rims, easily connected with cable ties to form a movable object that can be produced in a series on the spot. The aim of the manual is to set up an open process rather than to show how to design a product or final image. By involving the public, several functions of the dodecahedron can be envisioned; for instance, a wind play, a garden fence, or even a one-man pod. This allows participants to experience different perspectives of a wasteland and transform themselves from observers to designers. Furthermore, it visualises possibilities of the use and interpretation of unplanned space in a city."

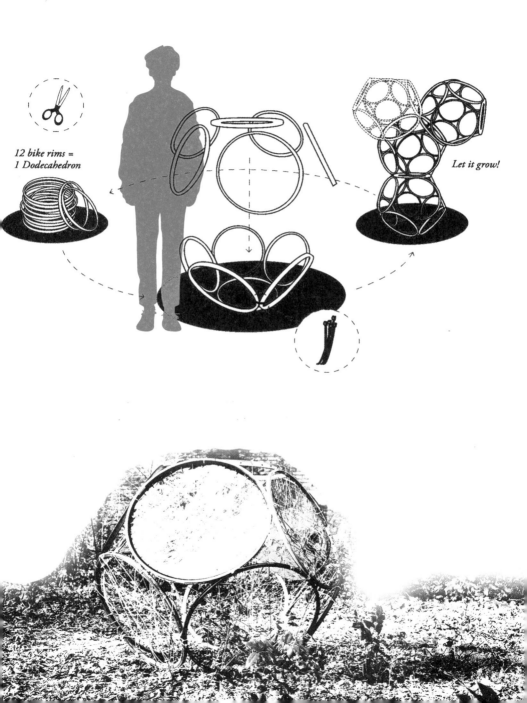

12 bike rims =
1 Dodecahedron

Let it grow!

DON'T BE AFRAID OF THE ART OF PARTICIPATION

Benjamin Foerster-Baldenius

There are many words for it and not all of them start with co: coauthorship, collaboration, cooperation, acting together, working collectively, co-working, direct democracy, open source, flat hierarchy, shared economy, community activity, teamwork, open ears, grassroots, bottom-up organisation, anarchy, swarm intelligence, consumer orientation, mediation, compromising, and the worst: participation. Some sound trendy, others old-school; some have associations to the 70s and hippies; others are more related to the squatters movement of the 90s; and some are clearly here and now. You can easily imagine the words written with chalk in some cheesy font on a blackboard in one of the gentrified hipster quarters around the world, or on the side of a small fast BMW. They all have a slightly different meaning and they all look at the same phenomenon from slightly different angles, but at heart they have something in common: the search for a common ground.

If you look at this world of togetherness from the outside— say from the position of a solitary working author of books or artworks or architecture or scenography—all these political, moral, religious, and economic motivations for participation must look like a nightmare: people standing barefoot in a circle and holding hands before they discuss what to do together, only able to leave if everyone truly feels they've truly come to a consensus. But these kinds of assemblies take forever with no conclusion, so everyone frustratedly hops into their sun-powered electro city car to bury the unrest of their souls in the compost soil of their community gardens. Still, in your dreams, you scream: "No! I will never take part in this".

Between all the good rational reasons to start a fruitful exchange of cultural values, there is one that sticks out like a lighthouse: collaboration can be fun! It makes us happy because it makes sense. It just needs A) the right training, B) the right people, and C) the right words.

174 A) If we spend six years at a University strangling our own little minds to learn how to present a coherent and unique concept, we cannot imagine that by working together, by asking the right experts, it is possible to be more experimental, faster, stronger, cheaper, and more coherent with the results of our work than anyone else. And we find it hard to believe that losing the authorship of a work can be extremely productive.

B) The main obstacle is to find the right people to collaborate with. Not during the learning process—here, everyone still knows it's more fun to hang out and invent something together— but after, out there in the real world where people do not believe anymore in the power of co-....

C) Participation describes a process of an author who invites others into his process. This model, of course, must fail. Collaboration means learning to communicate with a common language—drawing, for example—without a hidden agenda.

We all work in cities (and cities are everywhere) and we should all aim to make them better places. In doing so, we should not need to force ourselves to ask local experts what is the most neces- sary pressing subject in their neighbourhood: we know they know better. But we also know we are experts, too. And that locals need us as we need them. So we collaborate.

Collaboration is not our religion—it's not our way to make more money, faster—but maybe it is a moral act. We cannot solve all the problems in our cities alone, we cannot rely on politicians, governments, and the free market: we need small, strong, innova- tive, and altruistic communities that take their share of responsi- bility. Collaboration is a matter of trust: no trust, no city. But first of all it's our language: a language to learn. And, as with every language, as soon as you speak it fluently, it's fun to use. Participate now!

Concept + Publisher

Dan Dorocic is a practicing architect and member of design & architecture collective ON/OFF from the early days. Through his involvement with ON/OFF, he has been focusing on mobile architecture, publishing, and pedagogical workshops. Dan also occasionally works on more traditional architecture projects and has curated several exhibitions and run workshops and taught in architecture departments in Germany and Norway.

Onomatopee Projects, founded in 2006 and directed by Freek Lomme since, is a curating and editorially led public gallery and publisher that is particularly known for their self-initiated and transdisciplinary projects. Furthermore, they also host the projects of progressive individuals as well as artist-run and institutional organisations.

ON/OFF is a network of designers, architects, curators, filmmakers, and urbanists. Our curiosity lies in the city and its processes. This complexity offers the basis for experiments into our contemporary condition and gives us the opportunity to question, to tune into, and to discover new realities. With each project we draw on our combined experiences and unique skills to investigate and affect the city's lived dimension. We primarily conceive of tools —structures both physical, social, and fictional—which enable shared engagement with the citizens of the place where the experiments are carried out.

Writers

Kim Dovey is an Australian architectural critic and Professor of Architecture and Urban Design at the University of Melbourne, Australia, teaching urban design theory. His book Framing Places (2nd ed. 2008) explores theories of place as mediators of power, incorporating case studies of politics of public space, housing, shopping malls, and corporate towers.

Nick Green has been a member of ON/OFF since its formation. He has collaborated on a number of projects with the group including the Kopf Kino installation, initiated as part of the 2012 Istanbul Design Biennial and subsequently exhibited widely across Europe. He also regularly contributes to ON/OFF's ongoing Conference Call project, taking part in the series of discussions with young design collectives internationally. Nick currently contributes to the collective remotely, working from London.

179 Fiona Shipwright is a writer and editor, originally from London, based in Berlin since 2014. A founding member of the &beyond collective, between 2014–2016 she was an editor for uncube magazine. She has also worked on editorial projects with Phaidon Press, Ruby Press, transmediale and raumlabor. As well as co-founding the discursive format series Way Too Concrete, exploring aspects of spatial production and representation, Fiona has written for The Architectural Review, PORT, rhizome, The Wire, Eye on Design and mono.kultur. She is currently working at Haus der Kulturen der Welt as Online Editor of anthropocene.curriculum.org.

Michael Maginness is an architectural designer and urbanist working across Australia and Europe. His research interests lie at the political intersection between the city, space and aesthetics. His design practice focuses on developing everyday spatial strategies in the struggle for the right to the city. Michael lives in Berlin and is a member of design collective ON/OFF.

Alison Hugill is a writer, editor and independent curator based in Berlin. She has a BA in Philosophy (King's College, Canada, 2009) and a Master's in Contemporary Art Theory (Goldsmiths College, University of London, 2011). Her research focuses on marxist-feminist politics, architecture, participatory design and aesthetic theories of community. Alison is Editor-in-Chief of Berlin Art Link magazine and a regular contributor to Artforum, Momus, Archinect, Artsy, Rhizome, AQNB, Sleek Magazine, Digital Icons, and ArtMargins, among other publications. Recent curatorial projects include: Future Ruins exhibition, Bergen, Norway (2013), In Reserve: On the Architecture of the Reservoir, Bauhaus Dessau, Germany (2014), Hardbakka Ruins Project, Bergen, Norway (2014-17), Blacklisted exhibition at Seoul Art Space Geumcheon (2016). She is one half of design collective antiforum and a host of Berlin Community Radio intersectional feminist talk show Hystereo.

Diane Barbé is dedicated to exploring human and non-human worlds through sound, and integrates multidisciplinary artistic practices, education and research in her work. In 2020, she launched the LYRA floating house residency space in the bay of Rummelsburg in Berlin, which highlights the ecological and spatial tensions of the area while proposing an alternative art space. As a sound artist, Diane performs live with electronic and wind instruments and curates a series of experimental music events called Oneironautics. For three years, she was an associate researcher at the Chair for International Urbanism and Design at the TU Berlin, co-organising a major bilateral exchange

180 programme on urban heritage in Dar es Salaam (Tanzania) and Berlin. Currently training as a documentary recordist and sound designer at the Universität der Künste Berlin, Diane cultivates future imaginaries in her multichannel installations and proposes immersive listening experiences that weave fiction and realism together.

Samuel Días Carvalho is a founding member of ON/OFF and has been an active member since its foundation, developing projects in the intersection between art, design and public space. He is a guest tutor at Chalmers University of Technology, in the course "Design for Social Inclusion" and "Dare 2 Build", focusing on urban space in public housing estates on the periphery of Gothenburg. Since 2019 he works for the City Planning Office of Gothenburg as project architect in "Place Building".

Benjamin Foerster-Baldenius studied architecture in Berlin (TU Berlin / HDK) and Copenhagen (Kgl.Kunstakademie). He received the Max Taut Prize for the best diploma thesis, the 1997 Foundation of the "Institute of Applied Architecture". Since then, he has been artistic director of many projects for raumlaborberlin. He was a professor for architecture at the Academy of Art, Architecture and Design Prague (VSUP) in 2010/12; the Kunsthochschule Weißensee in the master study programme Raumstrategien 2014/15; and Professor of transdisciplinary design of the Folkwang University of the Arts in Essen.

Dan Dorocic is a member of design & architecture collective ON/OFF and has been an active member since its foundation. More recently through ON/OFF, he has been focusing on mobile architecture, publishing, and pedagogical workshops. Dan also works on more traditional architecture projects and has participated in curating a few of exhibitions, as well as teaching in Germany and Norway.

Editors

Dan Dorocic is a member of design & architecture collective ON/OFF and has been an active member since its foundation. More recently through ON/OFF, he has been focusing on mobile architecture, publishing, and pedagogical workshops. Dan also works on more traditional architecture projects and has participated in curating a few of exhibitions, as well as teaching in Germany and Norway.

181 Alison Hugill is a writer, editor and independent curator based in Berlin. She has a BA in Philosophy (King's College, Canada, 2009) and a Master's in Contemporary Art Theory (Goldsmiths College, University of London, 2011). Her research focuses on marxist-feminist politics, architecture, participatory design and aesthetic theories of community. Alison is Editor-in-Chief of Berlin Art Link magazine and a regular contributor to Artforum, Momus, Archinect, Artsy, Rhizome, AQNB, Sleek Magazine, Digital Icons, and ArtMargins, among other publications. Recent curatorial projects include: Future Ruins exhibition, Bergen, Norway (2013), In Reserve: On the Architecture of the Reservoir, Bauhaus Dessau, Germany (2014), Hardbakka Ruins Project, Bergen, Norway (2014-17), Blacklisted exhibition at Seoul Art Space Geumcheon (2016). She is one half of design collective antiforum and a host of Berlin Community Radio intersectional feminist talk show Hystereo.

Ane Crisan was born in Carei, Romania in 1991. Studied architecture in Timisoara and Naples between 2009 - 2015. Worked at different architecture /urban planning offices in Timisoara, Amsterdam and Berlin. During her school years, she coordinated a sociological and urban design workshop as part of StudentFest Timisoara and was part of Theatre Festival in her hometown. Currently based in Berlin, she is working as a freelance architect with artistic contribution focusing on stage design and art installations in collaboration with office Awst & Walther. She designed our world-traveling guy, some maps and other aspects of this book.

Halina Rachelson studied at University of British Columbia. She spent a few months in Berlin and Delft in the summer of 2016 where she worked on this book and other projects with ON/OFF in Berlin.

Josh Plough is a writer, editor and curator who specialises in building networks of investigative and critical people around a subject. Now in Warsaw, he's in the process of founding the art and design theory bookshop and hosting space Ziemniakii.

Cover Design

Mike Ellis is a Toronto-based artist and co-founder of 156 Studio. Mike's powerful illustrations have landed him in The New York Times, The New Yorker, and Wired, among many other fine publications.

Anika Juliane Neubauer is an architectural designer and researcher based in Berlin. Since 2013 she holds a position as Assistant Professor at the Architecture Department / TU Braunschweig. Together with the well known landscape architect Gabriele G. Kiefer she released the publication "Landscape for Architects" about strategies in understanding and teaching landscape urbanism. Her professional work focuses on graphic design and conceptual planning. Anika is founder of the concept agency ANICOWORKING.COM and a permanent member of ON/OFF.

Co-machine Designers

Melissa Jin currently uses an iPhone 6s with a RhinoShield case, having previously owned an iPhone 5c (stolen), an iPhone 4 (lost) and a Nokia 7360. At present, she has 4984 photos, 120 videos and 1837 unread emails. Her 55 apps, laid out according to icon colour and ease of access, are divided between 3 home screens. Apps used on a daily basis include WhatsApp, Messenger, Facebook, Google Maps and SleepCycle. She dabbles with Instagram, but rarely uses Snapchat and has difficulty navigating within the app, though she finds the filter function highly amusing. Growing up in Brisbane, Singapore and Wuhan has largely shaped her views of the world, and these days, she is exploring the incoherence of the city of Brussels.

Ahmad S. Khouja is founder and principal designer at DAMJ design+craft. He has studied and worked in the US and UK before moving to Beirut. Ahmad has worked in architecture, furniture design, multimedia installations, parametric-consulting, and digital-fabrication. He often finds inspiration from the crafts discovered in his native Damascus while tagging along with his mother during her antique trading. Other than the designs done through DAMJ, Ahmad's interests lie in the intersection of craft and public space, where he has designed urban guerrilla-survival machines. He is a graduate of Columbia and UC Berkeley Universities and has taught design and parametric modelling at LAU and AUB in Lebanon.

Kaegh Allen is an international designer and architect currently based in the Netherlands. He holds degrees in Architecture from Oxford Brookes University and TU Delft and has worked professionally in Paris, Berlin, and Amsterdam. Kaegh has most recently focused more on making and building and has led design workshops for EASA festival in Lithuania and at Buurman material workshop in Rotterdam, as well as building his own designs. His interests lie in alternative forms of building: Architecture is just one of those forms.

The Office of Urban Play is Edwina Portocarrero, a PhD candidate at MIT's Media Lab, and designs hybrid physical/digital objects for play, education and performance. Living between analog and digital, hand-crafted and mass-produced, her work explores the ways in which objects and materials mediate and augment experience across contexts and cultures.

Tyler Stevermer is an architectural designer, editor, researcher, and educator based in San Francisco. He holds a master of architecture from MIT. Stevermer's work investigates new and historic methodologies for occupant-based design processes, material driven forms/spatialities, and innovative workplace design for technology clients. Exquisite Triciclo (and other Networked Playscapes) was produced with the help of numerous others known as The Office of Urban Play.

RealLabor is Thomas Rustemeyer (*1984, Freiburg): Architectural studies at Karlsruhe Institute of Technology (KIT) and University of the Arts, Berlin (UdK); Academic staff at the department of scenography and exhibition design of Karlsruhe University of Arts and Design (HfG); Scenographer, architect and urbanist, Studiorustemeyer, Karlsruhe.

Marius Gantert (* 1984, Heidelberg): Architectural studies at Karlsruhe Institute of Technology (KIT) and Interdisciplinary Urban Design graduate studies, University College London (UCL); Academic staff at the institute of landscape planning and ecology, Stuttgart University and project coordinator for the research project 'Realworld Laboratory for Sustainable Mobility Culture". Architect and urbanist with Teleinternetcafe, Berlin. The project was realised with Theater Rampe, Stuttgart and Lastenrad Stuttgart.

Office for Political Innovation is a Madrid/New York-based practice directed by Andrés Jaque which develops architectural projects that bring inclusivity into daily life. All their architectures can be seen as durable assemblages of the diversity ordinary life is made of.

PINKCLOUD.DK is an award-winning ideas laboratory founded in 2011 by four international designers. We excel at developing concepts and strategies that address a range of challenges from our clients,

184 communities, and environments. We have no predeter-
mined solution, but treat every project as a unique exercise
in design thinking. Our process identifies the underlying
challenges of any project with precise analysis, combined with design
intuition and rational problem-solving to create an implementable
holistic strategy of action. Our expertise lies in: visioning, conceptual
strategy and development including branding, product design, interactive design, architecture and urban-scale planning.

Philipp von Hase is a wood-oriented designer and maker based in
Bergen, Norway. On one hand, he works with sculptural Scandinavian
furniture design and, on the other hand, he is interested in inventing
Co-machines, prototypes and experiments that activate urban
space.

Marcos L. Rosa is an architect and urban planner (Faculdade de
Arquitetura e Urbanismo na Universidade de São Paulo, 2005). He
received with the highest honours (Suma cum laude) the title of
Doctor by the Technical University of Munich in Regional Planning and
urban design (2015). In 2015, he received his Doctoral degree with
the highest honours from the Technical University in Munich, later
published in open format in January 2016 by the TUM, and registered
in the German National Library. For his PhD, he received one of the full
"High level scholarships for young professionals and postgraduate
students from Latin America" from the European Union (through the
Alßan programme). His work includes research, teaching and design,
with focus in collaborative work, the editing of existing structures
and the redevelopment of existing structures and situations.

ConstructLab is the description of a collaborative construction practice working on both ephemeral and permanent projects. Unlike the
conventional architectural process in which the architect designs
and the builder builds, in ConstructLab a project's conception and
construction are brought together. The designer builds and continues
to design on site.

Íñigo Cornago & Claudia Sánchez are a studio dedicated to
researching and carrying out projects around urban space, architecture, and design. Their Cocook project has been selected for international exhibitions and projects around the city and public space. With
the band of architects, Los Bandidos, the studio works to promote 72
Hour Urban Action Madrid 14, the Spanish edition of the first international architectural competition in real time, framed within the Plan
for the Improvement of Urban Landscape District of Usera.

185 Rachel Peachey and Paul Mosig have been collaborating for several years, using photography, video, textiles, sculpture, and found objects to look at human/environment relationships. Their design studio, Racket, is based in The Blue Mountains of Australia. They specialise in unique and beautiful work for web & print, working with clients across Australia and around the world.

SolidOperations is an artistic practice based in Vienna, operating on spatial strategies and design. We care for big issues as well as for small problems regarding local constellations, design questions, or global problems. We fancy execution, sloppy or precise, and like to be involved in the whole process, from design to production, as closely as possible. We passionately misuse existing objects and materials to shape new designs. When we're not co-twerking in Vienna's cellars, we're scribbling sketches, preparing material, or cooking together.

Precious Plastic was started in 2013 by Dave Hakkens and is now in its third iteration, counting on dozens of people working on the project, remotely or on site (somewhere below sea level in the Netherlands). Precious Plastic is a global community of hundreds of people working towards a solution to plastic pollution. Knowledge, tools and techniques are shared online, for free.

Guerilla Architects is an international group of architects working on the forgotten and unused resources of our cities. Guerilla Architects work to uncover the hidden potential of our society. We develop flexible concepts based on a design process in order to reveal and preserve special qualities. Our strategy is to newly define spaces or open-sources independent of any previous function with consideration for the specific atmosphere of a place – Genius Loci – and its history.

Jason Vigneri-Beane is a founding partner of Planetary ONE and the founding principal of Split Studio. In addition, he is Coordinator of Pratt Institute's MS ARCH program, GAUD Digital Media and the GAUD Rome programme. He teaches the post-professional thesis sequence, design studios, and media courses. His work currently explores the design-research potential of near-future scenario planning, techno-social change, and speculative relationships among architecture, ecology, and industrial design. He has taught and lectured in Europe, Asia, and North America.

Karin Blomberg is a Swedish visual artist based in Bergen, Norway, whose practice focuses mainly on site-specific installation. She holds a MA in fine art from Bergen Academy of Art and Design. Her work was shown at the Norwegian national exhibition Høstustillingen 2016 in Oslo, where her piece "Gjennomgang" was awarded Norwegian Association of Art Societies debutant prize. In collaboration with Erna E. Skúladóttir, Blomgren has presented large, spatial installations at Galleri F15, KRAFT, and Visningsrommet USF in Norway.

Joel Kerner is a registered architect and educator based in Chicago and L.A.. His practice navigates the polemical and the pragmatic while engaging in broader design discourse through exhibitions, workshops, lectures, and publications. He has held teaching positions with the Southern California Institute of Architecture and Judson University's School of Art, Design, and Architecture, where he is an adjunct professor, recurring critic, and workshop host. His work has been exhibited and published in the U.S., France, Iran, Norway, and Estonia.

Tal Mor Sinay is a self-employed industrial designer, working with a number of companies and organisations in the fields of consumer electronics, furniture and lighting, fashion, agriculture markets, spacial and exhibition design.

Andrea Orving is a Copenhagen-based architect and designer with a Master's from the Royal Danish Academy for Fine Art and Architecture.

Atelier Slant is a multicultural group of young architects and designers based in Berlin, interested in experimental, alternative ways of thinking, creating and living. Riccardo Torresi is an Italian architect experienced in sustainable design and media art. Giulia Domeniconi is an Italian architect with experience in wooden structures and temporary architecture. Yazan Tabaza is a Jordanian graphic designer and media artist interested in different ways of living and falafels. Irene Frassoldati is an architect and engineer from Italy with a solid experience in building structures. Mirko Gatti is an Italian architect specialised in furniture design and with a great passion for camping.

Alex v. Lenthe is a Berlin-based architect currently working for AFF-architects. He received his Bachelor of Architecture at TU Berlin and now studies at Universität der Künste Berlin.

Takehito Etani invents fantastical wearable devices and installations that he refers to as spiritual prosthetics. He explores the relationships between body, consciousness, and technology in contemporary daily life. His subtly humorous performances with such devices are intended as both social critique and a vision of a future alternative reality. Etani was born in Japan and lives and works in Oakland, California.

The Interactive Architecture Lab is a multi-disciplinary studio interested in the Behaviour and Interaction of Things, Environments, and their Inhabitants. We design, build, and experiment with Responsive Environments, Robotics and Kinetic Structures, Multi-Sensory Interfaces, Wearable Computing and Prosthetics, the Internet of Things, Performance and Choreography.

Julia Klauer is a Berlin-based Spatial Designer with interest in urban processes. In 2015, she finished her Master in Visual Communication at the University of the Arts Berlin, focussing on exhibition design. During a semester abroad in Rotterdam in 2013, her interest in urban space began: since then she has participated on several projects like raumlaborberlin's "Osthang Project 2014" in Darmstadt (and designed the publication about it afterwards) and "picnic urbanism in Lichtenberg" by lived space lab. She joined On/Off to the summer school Hardbakka Ruins in Bergen and the Urban School Ruhr to Athens. Construction de l'Association was the result of her Master's thesis.

Alex Bruce is an architect that wanders the gridded streets of Philadelphia in pursuit of forgotten paths, edges, and landmarks that divulge the recalcitrant spirit of the city. He is captivated by the influences of geographical environments on the emotions and behaviour of people in public places. He strives to incorporate these insights into his professional pursuits of designing energetic, culturally-sensible and environmentally-sustainable, affordable housing communities. Aside from architecture, Alex is enthusiastic about piano, live music, graphic design and art.

Atilla Ali Tan was raised in Istanbul and completed his undergraduate studies with distinction at the Istanbul Technical University and postgraduate studies at the Bartlett, UCL. He primarily focuses on the relationship between cities, society and technology with a fascination for dynamic spatial productions and speculative urbanisms. He delivers these research and design topics through 3D modelling, filmmaking and installations. He has founded AAT_a in 2015. AAT_a is an architectural design company providing services for built structures, installations, products and interiors; specialising in design development, BIM implementation, graphics and visualisations.

188 Leonard Daisuke Yui is an Assistant Professor of Architecture at Roger Williams University in Bristol, Rhode Island. He is a Sustainable Studies minor core faculty and is a member of the Sustainable Grounds committee. He is a licensed architect and a LEED accredited professional. His research and teaching interest resides in the intersection of architecture and landscape and he holds post-professional degrees in Landscape Architecture and Architecture, as well as an Ecological Design certificate from the University of Oregon. He received is Bachelor's of Architecture from Cal Poly, San Luis Obispo.

Sahoko Yui's interests are in food waste, design, and sustainability research. Her dissertation investigates the role of attitudes and behaviours, environmental design, and community participation in waste reduction, with a focus on restructuring waste management strategies and practices at the local level. The goal of her practice is to work with various campus organisations, such as Project Compost and UC Davis Dining Services, to reduce food waste and its negative impacts. She was recently appointed as a member of the UC Davis compost expansion committee, the group is committed to providing better food waste management infrastructure and policies at UC Davis.

Niklas Fanelsa is a young architecture practice from Berlin. We work on private projects, public buildings, exhibitions and publications. The atelier was founded by Niklas Fanelsa in 2016. He studied architecture with Anne-Julchen Bernhardt at RWTH Aachen University and Yoshiharu Tsukamoto at Tokyo Institute of Technology. He worked at De Vylder Vinck Taillieu in Gent, Belgium and Thomas Baecker Bettina Kraus Architekten in Berlin/Germany. He taught at the Chair of Housing at RWTH Aachen University, the Chair of Contextual Design at BTU Cottbus and is currently with the Chair of Housing at Bauhaus University Weimar.

place/making is driven by a team of Designers and Urbanists who share a multifaceted perspective on urban practices. We are planning and producing projects that actively seek to stimulate transformative processes that promote the transitions towards more integrative, resilient, and ultimately sustainable cities. We use design to understand, explain and mediate contexts and topics; to involve different actors and initiate innovative, participatory solutions; to document and publish our results and to obtain connectivity. A transdisciplinary, international, and intercultural background enables us to communicate complex ideas between experts and non-experts, across disciplines and knowledge cultures. place/making is based in Berlin and Tokyo and started in 2014. Our core team is complemented by associated practitioners in the fields of Architecture, Web-Development and Exhibition Design.

Stefanie Rittler is a Berlin-based social designer, carpenter and around-the-world explorer. Her focus lies in hands-on working on all kinds of materials from small to big scale in inconvenient spaces and social constellations. She is passionate about photography and graphics and happy to find little flea markets.

Jan Bernstein's artistic exploration gravitates toward scientific interests and physical experiments, using new technologies or academic research as sources and inspiration. He has been awarded multiple prizes and grants, including a Residency and Award by the European Digital Art and Science network in collaboration with ESO (European Southern Observatory), Jury Selection at the Japan Media Arts Festival, and an honorary mention at the Prix Ars Electronica. His work has been presented in international festivals, exhibitions, and galleries, such as in Ars Electronica Museum, CYNETART in Hellerau, galerie gerken in Berlin, Künstlerhaus Wien and The Modern Art Museum Santralistanbul in Istanbul.

umschichten is an artistic practice based in the Wagenhallen in Stuttgart (Germany). The studio uses temporary architecture as an approach for immediate action and creates built interventions in order to display local needs, ideas or passion. umschichten visualises theories, problems or a constellation of men and material by thinking about urban identities and the representation of different social and cultural groups in a city. They work fiercely on the borders of love and fear in the urban space.

Carole Frances Lung is an artist, activist, and scholar living in Long Beach, California. Through her alter ego Frau Fiber, Carole utilises a hybrid of playful activism, cultural criticism, research, and spirited crafting of one-of-a-kind garment production performances. She investigates the human cost of mass production and consumption, addressing issues of value and time through the thoroughly handmade construction and salvaging of garments. Her performances have been exhibited at Jane Addams Hull House Museum, Craft and Folk Art Museum, Museum of Contemporary Craft Portland, Sullivan Galleries, SAIC, Chicago IL, Ben Maltz Gallery, OTIS College of Art and Design, LA CA, Catherine Smith Gallery, Appalachian State University Boone NC and the Ghetto Biennale Port Au Prince Haiti.

Onomatopee 171
Co-machines:
Mobile Disruptive Architecture

ISBN: 978-94-93148-22-2

Concept and Production:
Dan Dorocic

Editors:
Alison Hugill and Josh Plough

Assistant Editor:
Halina Rachelson

Cover Image:
Mike Ellis

Illustrations:
Anika Neubauer

Photo credits:
p. 21 to 32: ON/OFF
p. 61 to 76: Ralph Roelse

Original Graphic Design:
Dan Dorocic, Anika Neubauer, Ane Crisan

Graphic Design and Art Direction for this Edition:
Wibke Bramesfeld

Printers:
Printon AS

Paper:
Cover: Umka color 250g/m^2
Inside: Munken Print Cream 115g/m^2,
Maxi Gloss 115g/m^2

Typeface:
GT Pressura Pro

ON/OFF
Published by Onomatopee

This publication was made possible thanks to the generous support of Provincie Noord-Brabant, Cultuur Eindhoven and Mondriaan Foundation.

Guerrilla Press Co-machine supported by the Bauhaus Dessau Stiftung

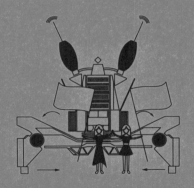

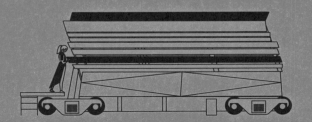

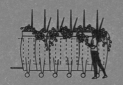

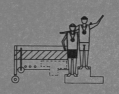

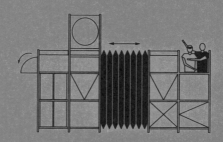